WOMEN'S WISDOM THROUGH THE AGES

Women's Wisdom through the Ages

Timeless Quotations on Life and Faith

Hodder & Stoughton
LONDON SYDNEY AUCKLAND

Copyright © 1994 by Harold Shaw Publishers

First published in Great Britain in 1995.
Reproduced by arrangement with Harold Shaw Publishers,
Box 567, Wheaton, IL 60189, USA.

Compiled by Mary Horner and Vinita Hampton Wright.

10 9 8 7 6 5 4 3 2 1

British Library Cataloguing in Publication Data
A record for this book is available from the British Library

ISBN 0 340 64240 8

Printed and bound in Great Britain by
Cox & Wyman Ltd, Reading, Berkshire

Hodder and Stoughton
A Division of Hodder Headline PLC
338 Euston Road
London NW1 3BH

Contents

Introduction

"She is clothed with strength and dignity;
she can laugh at the days to come.
She speaks with wisdom,
and faithful instruction is on her tongue."

So the book of Proverbs describes the woman of noble character.

She has always been with us, moulding the attitudes of both home and society. Throughout much of history, hers has been an anonymous contribution, silenced in cultures that denied her education or the right to voice her opinion in the public square.

Yet she has founded movements that cared for the poor, the sick, and imprisoned. She has composed books of poetry and prose, and written hymns. She has raised up sons like Jesus Christ, St. Augustine, and John Wesley, and has been the fountain of strength behind great men—men like John Adams, Louis XIV, and Martin Luther—who shaped world events. She has learned how to influence others without wielding great power, and, through her own suffering, how to comfort those who need hope and encouragement. She has a determined faith, a gritty sense of humour, sharp powers of discernment, and the courage to stand up for unpopular principles. She was the last to watch Jesus Christ die on the cross, and the first to see him resurrected.

The wise woman comes to us in many forms and has appeared in many places of the world. Her words are not easy to find in libraries, because often she has not been an orator or writer or famous person, but a wife, a worker, a woman who, in her ordinary day, through her work, relationships, and seasons of life, has hungered after God. Many of her words have survived, and just a few of them are collected here. May we learn from her and be inspired to live with courage and God's kind of love and wisdom.

Faith
and
Commitment

I have faith in thee, O my God, that thou wilt not leave me, that thou wilt not permit me to go astray; but wilt keep me in all inward thought, as well as in all outward word and action.—**Catherine of Genoa**

The spiritual man and woman can afford to take desperate chances, and live dangerously in the interests of their ideals; being delivered from the many unreal fears and anxieties which commonly torment us, and knowing the unimportance of possessions and of so-called success. —**Evelyn Underhill,** *The Life of the Spirit*

Father, whate'er of earthly bliss thy sov'reign will denies,
Accepted at thy throne of grace, let this petition rise.

Give me a calm, a thankful heart, from every murmur free;
The blessings of thy grace impart, and let me live to thee.

Let the sweet hope that thou art mine my path of
  life attend;
Thy presence thro' my journey shine, and crown my
  journey's end.
—**Anne Steele**

We may be perfectly sure of this, that the time of our need is the time of his closest and tenderest watchfulness. What would we think of a mother who should run away from her children the moment they got into trouble? And yet this hateful thing, which we would resent in any human mother, some of God's own children do not hesitate to ascribe to him!—**Hannah Whitall Smith**

Spirit in Paradise, pray thee plead
That I may follow thy fair, humble way,
In thought, in wish, in every holy deed.
—**Vittoria Colonna**

Dear Lord, I thank thee for all the trials, through which thou didst lead me, and by which thou didst prepare me to behold thy Glory. Thou hast never forsaken nor forgotten me.—**Katherine von Bora**

As soon as we begin, daughters, to conquer this little carcass, it will not bother us so much. . . . Try not to fear death and loss of health. Leave all to God, and let come what may come.—**Teresa of Avila**

I trust in the same powerful God, that his holy arm and power will carry me through, whatever he hath yet for me to do. . . . I know his faithfulness and goodness, and I have experienced his Love.—**Margaret Fell Fox**

My life is consecrated to God, to suffer for him, as well as to enjoy Him.—**Madame Jeanne Guyon**

May I adore the mystery I cannot comprehend. Help me to be not too curious in prying into those secret things that are known only to thee, O God, nor too rash in censuring what I do not understand.—**Susanna Wesley**

If a man doubts his way, Satan is always ready to help him to a new set of opinions.—**Lydia Maria Child**

After we had spent a pleasant evening, my heart began to feel itself silenced before God and without looking at others, I felt myself under the shadow of the wing of God. . . . After the meeting my heart felt really light and as I walked home by starlight, I looked through nature up to nature's God.—**Elizabeth Fry**

I am a creature of God, and he has an undoubted right to do with me as seemeth good in his sight. I rejoice that I am in his hand—that he is everywhere present and can protect me in one place as well as in another.—**Ann Hasseltine Judson**

We plan—and God steps in with another plan for us and he is all-wise and the most loving friend we have always helping us.—**Nettie Fowler McCormick**

There are two things to do about the Gospel—believe it and behave it.—**Susanna Wesley**

God is never behind time.—**Mary Slessor**

When you get into a tight place and everything goes against you till it seems as though you could not hold on a minute longer, never give up, for that is just the place and time that the tide will turn.—**Harriet Beecher Stowe**

Whoso loves believes the impossible.—**Elizabeth Barrett Browning**

God can make you anything you want to be, but you have to put everything in his hands.—**Mahalia Jackson**

O my God! Imprint it on my soul with the strength of the Holy Spirit that, by his grace supported and defended, I may never more forget that thou art my all, and that I cannot be received in thy heavenly kingdom without a pure and faithful heart supremely devoted to thy holy will. Oh, keep me for the sake of Jesus Christ!—**Elizabeth Seton**

I am the Lord's servant. May it be to me as you have said.—**Mary,** mother of Jesus, Luke 1:38

When he asks for and receives our all, he gives in return that which is above price—his own presence. The price is not great when compared with what he gives in return; it is our blindness and our unwillingness to yield that make it seem great.—**Rosalind Goforth,** *How I Know God Answers Prayer*

When one door of happiness closes, another opens; but often we look so long at the closed door that we do not see the one which has been opened for us.—**Helen Keller,** from *The Faith of Helen Keller*

There was a man who had been for years trying to break up all the meetings, and had succeeded. He came to this meeting and commenced as usual. He talked about me and said all the wicked things he could think of. He did all he could to keep the people from coming to the altar. The brethren became discouraged, and said there was no mercy for him. I felt if he was ever saved it must be that night. I was very much impressed to pray to God to remove the stumbling block; if there was any mercy for him, to convert him at once, or remove him out of the way. . . . praises be to God for answering my prayer in sending conviction so deep that he was glad to cry for mercy. He said he believed that that prayer saved him. The next night I called on him to address the congregation. The people were very much surprised to see such a change. God can and will give us victory if we only trust him.—**Maria Woodworth-Etter**

I did not believe the story of Daniel in the lions' den until I had to take some of these awful marches [through the leopard forests of Nigeria]. Then I knew it was true, and that it was written for my comfort.—**Mary Slessor**

May we not allow our hearts to wander away, for life can be so empty and futile without Jesus.—**Ann Kiemel Anderson,** *First Love*

If I am not in God's grace, may God bring me there; if I am in it, may he keep me there.—**Joan of Arc**

I resolve to keep God in my thoughts and heaven in my view.—**Sarah Kirby Trimmer**

Let me have but one wish, that of pleasing thee; but one fear, the fear of offending thee.—**Elizabeth Seton**

No coward soul is mine,
No trembler in the world's storm-troubled
    sphere:
I see heaven's glories shine,
And faith shines equal, arming me from fear.
—**Emily Brontë**

For us . . . Whatever's undergone,
Thou knowest, willest what is done,
Grief may be joy misunderstood:
Only the Good discerns the good.
I trust thee while my days go on!
—**Elizabeth Barrett Browning**

Lord Jesus Christ, our God, the worries and cares of our lives beat up against us in great waves. Help us to see thee walking over the surging waters.—**Princess Ileana of Romania**

As a Christian, I hope I can lead the kind of life that makes others look at me and say, "What's missing in my life that she has?" That's a greater testimony than anything I can say.—**Marilyn Quayle**

Lord, whilst my fleeting time shall last,
Thy Goodnes let me Tell.
And new Experience I have gain'd,
My future Doubts repell.
—**Anne Bradstreet**

I do believe that God has answers for some and peace of mind for others when answers do not come, and that, one way or another, God . . . has the very best idea of how to bring sense to all the chaos of shattered dreams we see around us.—**Jill Briscoe,** *Heartbeat*

There is not a guarantee in the world. Oh your needs are guaranteed, your needs are absolutely guaranteed by the most stringent of warranties, in the plainest, truest words: knock; seek; ask. But you must read the fine print. "Not as the world giveth, give I unto you."—**Annie Dillard,** *Pilgrim at Tinker Creek*

What people don't realize is how much religion costs. They think faith is a big electric blanket, when of course it is the cross.—**Flannery O'Connor,** *The Habit of Being*

Because we cannot see the hand of God in our affairs, we rush to the conclusion that he has lost sight of them and of us. We look at the "seemings" of things instead of at the underlying facts, and declare that, because God is unseen, He must necessarily be absent. And especially is this the case if we are conscious of having ourselves wandered away from him and forgotten him. We judge him by ourselves, and think that he must have also forgotten and forsaken us. We measure his truth by our falseness, and find it hard to believe he can be faithful when we know ourselves to be so unfaithful.—**Hannah Whitall Smith**

It appears that God has deliberately left us in a quandary about many things. Why did he not summarize all the rules in one book, and all the basic doctrines in another? He could have eliminated the loopholes, prevented all the schisms over morality and false teaching that have plagued his Church for two thousand years. Think of the squabbling and perplexity we would have been spared. And think of the crop of dwarfs he would have reared! —**Elisabeth Elliot,** *The Liberty of Obedience*

I gave to God what belonged to him, and God kept [for] us what was thine and mine.—**Elizabeth of Hungary**

Teresa and this money are indeed nothing; but God, Teresa, and four ducats can accomplish the thing.—**Teresa of Avila**

I have on occasion told my agnostic friends, who don't understand the certainty I have about God's existence and love for me, I could sooner doubt their existence than that of a Person with whom I have been speaking daily for forty years.—**Ruth A. Schmidt,** from *Our Struggle to Serve*

Sitting there on my bed's edge, I raised both hands heavenward. "God, if there be a God," I whispered, for I was not going to believe in what did not exist just to get a mental opiate, "if you will prove to me that you are, and if you will give me peace, I will give you my whole life. I'll do anything you ask me to do, go where you send me, obey you all my days." Then I climbed into bed and pulled the blankets over me.—**Isobel Kuhn,** *By Searching*

Hilarion, the governor, who assumed power after the death of the proconsul Minucius Timinianus, said, "Have pity on your father's grey head; have pity on your infant son; offer sacrifice for the emperors' welfare." But I answered, "I will not." Hilarion asked, "Are you a Christian?" And I answered, "I am a Christian." And when my father persisted in his attempts to dissuade me, Hilarion ordered him thrown out, and he was beaten with a rod. My father's injury hurt me as much as if I myself had been beaten, and I grieved because of his pathetic old age. Then the sentence was passed; all of us were condemned to the beasts. We were overjoyed as we went back to the prison cell. Since I was still nursing my child who was ordinarily in the cell with me, I quickly sent the deacon Pomponius to my father's house to ask for the baby, but my father refused to give him up. Then God saw to it that my child no longer needed my nursing, nor were my breasts inflamed. After that I was no longer tortured by anxiety about my child or by pain in my breasts.—**Perpetua**

Worry does not empty tomorrow of its sorrow, it empties today of its strength. It does not enable us to escape evil. It makes us unfit to face evil when it comes. It is the interest you pay on trouble before it comes.—**Corrie ten Boom,** *Clippings from My Notebook*

Earth's crammed with heaven,
And every common bush afire with God;
But only he who sees, takes off his shoes,
The rest sit round it and pluck blackberries.
—**Elizabeth Barrett Browning**

In this time of confusion we took Walter's friend, Pastor Fuchs, into our confidence. We confessed our doubts as to how our lives might fit together in the future. "A Christian," he answered simply, "is one who can wait." And so, more or less reconciled to waiting, we said good-bye. I returned to Paris and packed my trunks for Africa. Our love was strong and deep, but we did not know when, where—or even if—we would ever meet again.—**Ingrid Trobisch,** *On Our Way Rejoicing*

I love to tell the story
Of unseen things above,
Of Jesus and his glory,
Of Jesus and his love.
I love to tell the story,
Because I know 'tis true;
It satisfies my longings
As nothing else can do.

I love to tell the story,
More wonderful it seems
Than all the golden fancies
Of all our golden dreams.
I love to tell the story,
It did so much for me;
And that is just the reason
I tell it now to thee.
—**A. Katherine Hankey**

I am too happy in this world to think much about the future, except to remember that I have cherished friends awaiting me there in God's beautiful Somewhere.—**Helen Keller**

We would see Jesus; the great rock foundation
Whereon our feet were set by sov'reign grace;
Not life nor death, with all their agitation,
Can thence remove us, if we see his face.
—**Anna B. Warner,** "We Would See Jesus; for the Shadows"

Be not perplexed,
Be not afraid,
Everything passes,
God does not change.
Patience wins all things.
He who has God lacks nothing;
God alone suffices.
—**Teresa of Avila**

Devotional
Life

Begin and end the day with him who is the Alpha and Omega, and if you really experience what it is to love God, you will redeem all the time you can for his more immediate service.—**Susanna Wesley**

When a man spins evermore on his own axis, like a child's toy I saw the other day . . . what is the use of him but to make a noise? No greater tormentor is there, than self-love . . . even to self.—**Elizabeth Barrett Browning**

I have never seen anyone who I thought had committed more sin than I. . . . I never saw the corruption of but one life, one heart—that was mine. I was never so shocked, so disgusted, so disgraced with remorse over any life so much as my own. My heart was the foulest place I ever saw.—**Carry Nation**

I wouldn't spend much time worrying about dryness. It's hard to steer a path between indifference and presumption and [there's] a kind of constant spiritual temperature-taking that don't do any good or tell you anything either.
—**Flannery O'Connor**, *The Habit of Being*

The sight with which the soul is endowed by nature is Charity. This sight has two eyes: love and reason. Reason can see God only in what he is not; love rests not except in what he is.—**Hadewijch of Antwerp**

It seems to me that there is in each of us a capacity to comprehend the impressions and emotions which have been experienced by mankind from the beginning. This inherited capacity is a sort of sixth sense—a soul-sense which sees, hears, feels, all in one.—**Helen Keller,** *The Story of My Life*

The fire of God's love must burn up self-love and self-will and let the soul appear, beautiful and full of grace, as it was meant to be when God created us.—**Catherine of Siena**

Don't let controversy hurt your soul. Live near to God by prayer. Just fall down at his feet and open your very soul before him, and throw yourself right into his arms. —**Catherine Booth**

Sincerity is never ludicrous; it is always respectable. —**Charlotte Brontë**

Then dearest Lord, keep me as I am, while I live, for this is true content, to hope for nothing, to desire nothing, expect nothing, fear nothing.—**Elizabeth Seton**

We must *be* good before we can *do* good; be real before we can accomplish real things. No generalized benevolence, no social Christianity however beautiful and devoted, can take the place of this centering of the spirit on eternal values; this humble, deliberate recourse to Reality.—**Evelyn Underhill,** *The Life of the Spirit*

God, of thy goodness, give me thyself; for thou art enough to me.—**Julian of Norwich**

We can choose to gather to our hearts the thorns of disappointment, failure, loneliness, and dismay due to our present situation, or we can gather the flowers of God's grace, unbounding love, abiding presence, and unmatched joy.—**Barbara Johnson,** *Stick a Geranium in Your Hat and Be Happy!*

Mythic moments are incidents in life, common to all of us though we mostly ignore them, so laden with truth they almost overkill meaning. They are pregnant with reality, ripe-bellied women, grotesquely overdue for delivery. Mythic moments knock at our inattention, part the fragile curtain of our illusion, demand by overstatement that we stare at truth.—**Karen Burton Mains,** *The Fragile Curtain*

Thou, the light, hast not regarded my darkness. Thou, true life, hast not regarded my living death. Thou, the physician, hast not been repelled by my grave infirmities. Thou, the eternal purity, hast not considered the many miseries of which I am full. Thou, who art the infinite, hast overlooked that I am finite. Thou, who art wisdom, hast overlooked my folly. Thy wisdom, thy goodness, thy clemency, thy infinite Good, have overlooked these infinite evils and sins, and the many others which are in me.—**Catherine of Siena**

I.
By night when others soundly slept,
And had at once both ease and rest,
My waking eyes were open kept,
And so to lye I found it best.

II.
I sought him whom my Soul did Love,
With tears I sought him earnestly;
He bow'd his ear down from Above,
In vain I did not seek or cry.

III.
My hungry Soul he fill'd with Good,
He in his Bottle putt my teares,
My smarting wounds washt in his blood,
And banisht thence my Doubts and feares.

IV.
What to my Saviour shall I give,
Who freely hath done this for me?
I'le serve him here whilst I shall live,
And Love him to Eternity.
—**Anne Bradstreet**

From silken self, O Captain free
Thy soldier, who would follow thee:
From subtle love of softening things,
From easy choices, weakenings,
From all that dims thy Calvary,
O Lamb of God, deliver me.
—**Amy Carmichael**

Humility is an "invisible grace"—those who possess it are
unaware of it.—**Penelope J. Stokes,** *Ruth & Daniel*

The present moment comes to every one fully charged
with God. To respond to him without flinching as he
comes in that moment—there to touch and accept his
Eternity, undeflected by self-will or self-love—this is sanc-
tity.—**Evelyn Underhill,** *Mixed Pasture*

The mind of a Christian should be always composed,
temperate, free from all extremes of mirth or sadness, and
always disposed to hear the voice of God's Holy Spirit.
—**Susanna Wesley**

I suppose I'm one of the few people who actually like
Lent. I like it in the same way I like throwing away last
year's student essays and clearing out my file cabinets.
During Lent some deep crack opens in my soul, down
which I like to shovel the dirt and debris that has accu-
mulated over the year. The sly self-deceptions, the
dogged willfulness, the witless pain I've left in my wake

that I've been too busy to notice or repair.—**Virginia Stem Owens**, from *Stories for the Christian Year*

Lord, you are my lover,
My longing,
My flowing stream,
My sun,
And I am your reflection.
—Mechthild of Magdeburg

As we begin to see the package God is putting together in our lives and discover his purposes for bringing us to our world, it will provide us with the framework we need to make wise choices. In addition, we will find that a sense of purpose gives hope in the midst of tragedy and difficulty, gives meaning to the mundane aspects of our lives, and helps us to make our lives count for God.—**R. Ruth Barton**, *Becoming Women of Purpose*

O my God, the contest they kept up with me, to hinder me from loving you, increased my love, and you yourself carried me away in an ineffable silence, when they hindered me from speaking to you. You united me so much the more powerfully to you, the more they tried to separate me.—**Madame Jeanne Guyon**

Imagination! who can sing thy force?
Or who describe the swiftness of thy course?
Soaring through air to find the bright abode,

Th' empyreal palace of the thund'ring God,
We on thy pinions can surpass the wind,
And leave the rolling universe behind:
From star to star the mental optics rove,
Measure the skies, and range the realms above.
There in one view we grasp the mighty whole,
Or with new worlds amaze th' unbounded soul.
—**Phillis Wheatley,** "On Imagination"

Besides pride, the desire to appear innocent is one of the most dangerous religious impulses of all. Not only do we conceal our problem with excuses and project it onto others; worse still, we make sure that our defects can never receive the treatment they require.—**Rebecca Manley Pippert,** *Hope Has Its Reasons*

Anger and/or selfishness make us petty and turn what was originally just a little chip on the shoulder into a great forest in which we hide lest we be taken advantage of. —**Gayle Roper,** *Who Cares?*

Be happy, but be happy through piety.—**Madame Anne Germaine de Staël**

Since my heart was touched at seventeen years old, I believe I never have awakened from sleep, in sickness or in health, by day or by night, without my first waking thought being, "how best I might serve my Lord."—**Elizabeth Fry**

Who is he, that all my faculties should thus obey him? Who is he that gives light in such darkness in a moment; who softens a heart that seemed made of stone; who gives the waters of sweet tears, where for a long time great dryness seems to have prevailed; who inspires these desires; who bestows this courage? What have I been thinking of? What am I afraid of? What is it? I desire to serve this my Lord; I aim at nothing else but his pleasure; I seek no joy, no rest, no other good than that of doing his will. I was so confident that I had no other desire, that I could safely assert it.—**Teresa of Avila**

This opening you made in my heart, which is continually inhaling, breathing, and sighing, is a mouth which tells you words which would kill the body, if it had to go through the senses, since everything comes to saying that I see You to be essentially Love! Love! Having made me sing this canticle which makes me find myself in You again and again, You render me mute.—**Marie of the Incarnation**

You are my understanding, and I shall know what it [pleases] you I should know. I shall not weary myself with further seeking, but I will abide in peace with your understanding, which holds possession of my mind. —**Catherine of Genoa**

I need nothing but God, and to lose myself in the heart of Jesus.—**Margaret Mary Alacoque**

God never stops taking the initiative in relating to us. He is continually reaching out to us—personally, presently in each of our lives. He still calls; he pokes around inside of people, making them ill at ease, restless to know him. He reveals dissatisfaction and sin; he shows his love and faithfulness. His invitation is Come, believe. Relating to God is the most exciting adventure in life!—**Gladys Hunt,** *Relationships*

All the spiritual writers of past generations have recognised this joy in God, and all of them have written concerning the stripping process that seems necessary to bring us to it. They have called this process by different names, some calling it "inward desolation," and some the "winter of the soul," . . . but all meaning one and the same thing; and that thing is the experience of finding all earthly joys stained or taken away, in order to drive the soul to God alone.—**Hannah Whitall Smith**

Just as Jesus found it necessary to sweep the money-changers from the Temple porch, so we ourselves need a lot of housecleaning.—**Dale Evans Rogers**

Christ himself came down and took possession of me . . . I had never foreseen the possibility of that, of a real contact, person to person, here below, between a human being and God . . . in this sudden possession of me by Christ, neither my sense nor my imagination had any part: I only felt in the midst of my suffering the presence of a love.—**Simone Weil**

A very strange and solemn feeling came over me as I stood there, with no sound but the rustle of the pines, no one near me, and the sun so glorious, as for me alone. It seemed as if I felt God as I never did before, and I prayed in my heart that I might keep that happy sense of nearness in my life.—**Louisa May Alcott**

Near the cross, a trembling soul,
Love and mercy found me;
There the bright and Morning Star
sheds its beams around me.
—**Fanny J. Crosby,** "Jesus, Keep Me Near the Cross"

While place we seek, or place we shun
The soul finds happiness in none;
But with a God to guide our way,
'Tis equal joy, to go or stay.
—**Madame Jeanne Guyon**

When the dream in our heart is one that God has planted there, a strange happiness flows into us. At that moment all of the spiritual resources of the universe are released to help us. Our praying is then at one with the will of God and becomes a channel for the Creator's always joyous, triumphant purposes for us and our world.—**Catherine Marshall,** *Beyond Our Selves*

Beauty and grace are performed whether or not we will or sense them. The least we can do is try to be there.—**Annie Dillard,** *Pilgrim at Tinker Creek*

O most beautiful form,
O sweetest fragrance of desirable delights,
we sigh for you always in our sorrowful banishment!
When may we see you and remain with you?

But we dwell in the world,
and you dwell in our mind;
we embrace you in our heart
as if we had you here with us.

You, bravest lion, have burst through the heavens.
You have destroyed death, and are building life
in the golden city.

Grant us society in that city,
and let us dwell in you. . . .
—**Hildegard of Bingen**

Your glory pours into my soul like sunlight against gold.
When may I rest with you, Lord?
My joys are manifold.
You garment yourself in my soul, and my soul is clothed
in you;
—**Mechtild of Magdeburg**

It is a pleasant thing to behold the light, but sore eyes are not able to look upon it; the pure in heart shall see God, but the defiled in conscience shall rather choose to be buried under rocks and mountains than to behold the presence of the Lamb.—**Anne Bradstreet**

But I think that for converts—indeed for all Christians— the acknowledgment of sin is not self-hatred at all, but the beginning of self-acceptance and (in the healthy sense) of self-love. The dialogue with God which begins with the confession of one's own failures is not depressing; it is liberating.—**Emilie Griffin,** *Turning*

Spiritual
Growth

If you have begun to act well, do not turn back through constraint of the enemy, for through your endurance, the enemy is destroyed. Those who put out to sea at first sail with a favorable wind; then the sails spread, but later the winds become adverse. Then the ship is tossed by the waves and is no longer controlled by the rudder. But when in a little while there is calm, and the tempest dies down, then the ship sails on again. So it is with us, when we are driven by the spirits who are against us; we hold to the cross as our sail and so we can set a safe course.—**Mother Syncletica**

Be still, my soul! the Lord is on thy side;
Bear patiently the cross of grief or pain;
Leave to thy God to order and provide;
In every change he faithful will remain.
Be still, my soul! thy best, thy heavenly Friend
Thro' thorny ways leads to a joyful end.

Be still, my soul! thy God doth undertake
To guide the future as he has the past.
Thy hope, thy confidence let nothing shake;
All now mysterious shall be bright at last.
Be still, my soul! the waves and winds still know
His voice who ruled them while he dwelt below.

Be still, my soul! the hour is hast'ning on
When we shall be forever with the Lord,
When disappointment, grief, and fear are gone,

Sorrow forgot, love's purest joys restored.
Be still, my soul! when change and tears are past,
All safe and blessed we shall meet at last.
—**Katharina A. von Schlegel**

Psychologists at present are much concerned to entreat us
to "face reality." . . . Yet this facing of reality can hardly be
complete if we do not face the facts of the spiritual life.
—**Evelyn Underhill,** *The Life of the Spirit*

I take my heart in my hand,
O my God, O my God,
My broken heart in my hand:
Thou hast seen, judge thou.
My hope was written on sand,
O my God, O my God:
Now let thy judgment stand—
Yea, judge me now.

This condemned of a man,
This marred one heedless day,
This heart take thou to scan
Both within and without:
Refine with fire its gold,
Purge thou its dross away—
Yea hold it in thy hold,
Whence none can pluck it out.

I take my heart in my hand—
I shall not die, but live—

Before thy face I stand;
I, for thou callest such:
All that I have I bring,
All that I am I give;
Smile thou and I shall sing,
But shall not question much.
—**Christina G. Rossetti**

Don't worry about what you do not understand of the
Bible. Worry about what you do understand but do not
live by.—**Corrie ten Boom,** *Clippings from My Notebook*

I have made many grievous mistakes. They were of the
head, not of the heart.—**Carry Nation**

Life scums the cream of beauty with Time's spoon,
And draws the claret-wine of blushes soon;
Then boils it in a skillet clean of youth,
And thicks it well with crumbled bread of truth;
Sets it upon the fire of life which does
Burn clearer much when Health her bellows blows;
Then takes the eggs of fair and bashful eyes,
And puts them in a countenance that's wise,
Cuts in a lemon of the sharpest wit—
Discretion as a knife is used for it.
A handful of chaste thoughts, double refined,
Six spoonsful of a noble and gentle mind,
A grain of mirth to give't a little taste,
Then takes it off for fear the substance waste,

And puts it in a basin of good health,
And with this meat doth Nature please herself.
—**Margaret Cavendish,** Duchess of Newcastle

My very soul was flooded with celestial light . . . for the
first time I realized that I had been trying to hold the world
in one hand and the Lord in the other.—**Fanny J. Crosby**

If you wish to possess finally all that is yours, give yourself
entirely to God.—**Hadewijch of Antwerp**

Here we learn to serve and give,
And, rejoicing, self deny;
Here we gather love to live,
Here we gather faith to die.

Pressing onward as we can,
Still to this our hearts must tend;
Where our earliest hopes began,
There our last aspirings end.
—**Elizabeth R. Charles**

What if God arranged things so that we would experience a mild jolt of pain with every sin, or a tickle of
pleasure with every act of virtue? . . . Would you obey
because you loved God? I don't think so. I think you'd
obey simply because you desired pleasure and not pain.
—**Joni Eareckson Tada**

When we can begin to take our failures non-seriously, it means we are ceasing to be afraid of them. It is of immense importance to learn to laugh at ourselves.—**Katherine Mansfield**

Suffering will come, trouble will come—that's part of life—a sign that you are alive. If you have no suffering and no trouble, the devil is taking it easy. You are in his hand. —**Mother Teresa**

Incline us, oh God!, to think humbly of ourselves, to be severe only in the examination of our own conduct, to consider our fellow-creatures with kindness, and to judge of all they say and do with that charity which we would desire from them ourselves.—**Jane Austen**

Many can speak well, but few can do well. We are better scholars in the Theory then the practice part, but he is a true Christian that is proficient in both.—**Anne Bradstreet**

Questions about the ministry of women today must be seen as part of the Church's continual pilgrimage as the people of God already called, chosen and gifted yet still flawed, sinful and disobedient. The choice we are faced with today seems to be whether or not to move forward toward God's ultimate purpose or to remain mired in the past and fearful of change.—**Roberta Hestenes,** *Women and Men in Ministry*

God doesn't build a fence around his children to protect us from the suffering common to all humanity. It is clear from the Bible and from the lives of Christians in every generation that God uses suffering in some form in the life of every believer.—**Martha Reapsome,** *Journey of a Lifetime*

My God, I choose the whole lot. No point in becoming a Saint by halves. I'm not afraid of suffering for your sake; the only thing I'm afraid of is clinging to my own will. Take it, I want the whole lot, everything whatsoever that is your will for me.—**Therese of Lisieux**

But we moderns are suffering from a weakening of poetic and imaginative courage. We have had our religious imaginations deflated, somehow, by the spiritual impoverishment of our times. We need a new burst of religious and literary daring—one that allows us to connect our experience to the dazzling metaphors of Scripture.—**Emilie Griffin,** from *Stories for the Christian Year*

We live under the illusion that if we can acquire complete control, we can understand God, or we can write the great American novel. But the only way we can brush against the hem of the Lord, or hope to be part of the creative process, is to have the courage, the faith, to abandon control.—**Madeleine L'Engle,** *Walking on Water*

In the beginning there are a great many battles and a good deal of suffering for those who are advancing towards God and afterwards, ineffable joy. It is like those who wish to light a fire; at first they are choked by the smoke and cry, and by this means obtain what they seek (as it is said: "Our God is a consuming fire"): so we also must kindle the fire in ourselves through tears and hard work.—**Mother Syncletica**

God wants us to know that the soul is a life, which life of goodness and grace will last in heaven without end, loving God, thanking God, praising God. And just as we were to be without end, so we were treasured and hidden in God, known and loved from without beginning. Therefore God wants us to know that the noblest thing ever made is humankind, and the fullest substance and the highest power is the blessed soul of Christ.—**Julian of Norwich**

There is a question whether faith can or is supposed to be emotionally satisfying. I must say that the thought of everyone lolling about in an emotionally satisfying faith is repugnant to me. I believe that we are ultimately directed Godward but that this journey is often impeded by emotion.—**Flannery O'Connor**

Why do we say no? In order to say yes to what really matters.—**Miriam Adeney**

We must not be astonished if the devils stir up all the
regions of their dominion against Apostolic souls. It is
because the Devil well knows that one soul of this kind,
once listened to, would destroy his empire.—**Madame
Jeanne Guyon**

Change interrupts my nesting habits, intrudes into my
comfort zone. Say the word change, and I freeze. I have
learned to live to the full—wherever I am—by simply
pretending I'll be there forever. Otherwise I'd never get
involved in a new project, or invest myself in someone's
life, or bother to contribute to a group.—**Jill Briscoe**,
Renewal on the Run

Here, before my eyes, is my God and my King, the mild
and merciful Jesus, crowned with sharp thorns; shall I,
who am only a vile creature, remain before him crowned
with pearls, gold, and precious stones, and by my crown
mock his?—**Elizabeth of Hungary**

I had been exposed at church to lots of Christians who
seemed to spend their energies on prohibitions. I'm sure
my present life wouldn't pass muster with many of those
dear, rigid souls at the church where I grew up, but they
no longer represent God to me. No one represents God to
me but God himself, and therein lies the freedom he promised.—**Eugenia Price**, *What Really Matters*

The soul on earth is an immortal guest,
compelled to starve at an unreal feast;
a pilgrim panting for the rest to come;
an exile, anxious for his native home.
—Hannah More

Let the wise not glory in their wisdom, for the demons are wiser than they; let the strong not glory in their strength, for animals are stronger than men; let not the rich glory in their riches, for sinners are generally richer than good people; but those who wish to glory, let them glory in the knowledge and recognition of God.—Marie of the Incarnation

To what shall I liken me, Lord? To a rose that is cut and left to dry up in the hand. It loses its perfume; but if it remains on the rosebush, it is always fresh and beautiful and keeps all its perfume. Keep me, Lord, to give me life in you.
—Mariam Baouardy

O, that my poor cold heart could catch a spark from others, and be as a flame of fire in the Redeemer's service! Some few instances of success, which God, in the riches of his mercy, has lately favored me with, have greatly comforted me during my season of affliction; and I have felt the presence of God in my soul in a very remarkable manner.—Lady Huntingdon

I came to know, after eight years. . . . that I had found the Christian religion, which was good enough for me; but I had not found Christ, who is the Life of the religion and the Light of every man that cometh into the world. —**Pandita Ramabai**

A Christian will find it cheaper to pardon than to resent. Forgiveness saves the expense of anger, the cost of hatred, the waste of spirits.—**Hannah More**

Christ's purposes towards me have been no less than that . . . I should put my feet, however weak and unworthy, into his bleeding footprints, and go with him where he would lead me, so that a lost world might be reached and saved.—**Emma Booth-Tucker**

It is very easy for some temperaments to be devotional. It is not easy for any temperament to be consistently loving, humble, and faithful in performing the daily duties of life.—**Evelyn Underhill,** *The Ways of the Spirit*

Be thou all in all to us; and may all things earthly, while we bend them to our growth in grace, dwell lightly in our hearts, so that we may readily, or even joyfully, give whatever thou dost ask for.—**Mary Carpenter**

Unless you suffer, you do not grow.—**Hadewijch of Antwerp**

There are a lot of things that only happen once. Remembering that simple fact will help us live through them.
—**Jill Briscoe,** *Renewal on the Run*

Lord, my earthly nature is stood before my eyes
like a barren field
which hath few good plants grown in it.
Alas, sweetest Jesus and Christ,
now send me the sweet rain of thy humanity
and the hot sun of thy living Godhead
and the gentle dew of the holy Spirit
that I may wail and cry out the aches of my heart.
—**Mechtild of Magdeburg**

I once was an outcast stranger on earth,
A sinner by choice, and an alien by birth;
But I've been adopted, my name's written down,
An heir to a mansion, a robe, and a crown.
—**Harriett E. Buell,** "My Father Is Rich in Houses and Lands"

Life isn't always what you want, but it's what you've got;
so, with God's help, CHOOSE TO BE HAPPY.—**Barbara
Johnson,** *Stick a Geranium in Your Hat and Be Happy!*

A genuine Christian ought to be alive all over, with a
depth and vitality of soul that makes shallow judgment
and prejudices impossible.—**Evelyn Underhill,** *Mixed
Pasture*

Like a river glorious is God's perfect peace,
Over all victorious in its bright increase;
Perfect, yet it floweth fuller every day,
Perfect, yet it groweth deeper all the way.
Stayed upon Jehovah, hearts are fully blest;
Finding, as he promised, perfect peace and rest.
—**Frances Ridley Havergal**

To yield again and again to the calls God gives us, to come up higher when we are humanly convinced we have gone as high as we can go, this takes a special kind of courage. After each miracle God works in our lives, we may be grateful, but we are inclined to shut the door after it, as though one or two miracles were all one could expect, or tolerate, in one lifetime. But the Lord, more often than not, has something else in mind for us. As soon as we have caught our breath, he is asking us to start climbing again.
—**Emilie Griffin,** *Turning*

One great mistake we make about temptations is to feel as if the time spent in enduring them was all lost time. Days pass, perhaps, and we have been so beset with temptations as to feel as if we had made no progress. But it often happens that we have been serving the Lord far more truly while thus "continuing with him" in temptation, than we could have done in our times of comparative freedom from it.—**Hannah Whitall Smith**

I have come upon the happy discovery that this life hid with Christ in God is a continuous unfolding.—**Eugenia Price**

Prayer
and
Praise

My soul glorifies the Lord
and my spirit rejoices in God my
Savior,
for he has been mindful
of the humble state of his servant.
From now on all generations will call
me blessed,
for the Mighty One has done great
things for me—
holy is his name.
—**Mary,** mother of Jesus, Luke 1:46-49

How prone we are to sin, how sweet were made
The pleasures, our resistless hearts invade!
Of all my crimes, the breach of all thy laws,
Love, soft bewitching love! has been the cause;
Of all the paths that vanity has trod,
That sure will soonest be forgiven of God;
If things on earth may be to heaven resembled,
It must be love, pure, constant, undissembled:
But if to sin perchance the charmer press,
Forgive, O Lord, forgive our trespasses.
—**Aphra Behn**

I don't often pray in words; but I said to the Lord, "Help
us all, and keep us for one another."—**Louisa May Alcott**

To praise God
On high,
Joyfully here below,
To be true to him,
Without betrayal,
This is a noble work indeed!
—Hadewijch of Antwerp

Now thank we all our God,
With heart and hands and voices
Who wondrous things hath done
in whom his world rejoices.
—Catherine Winkworth

The train was on time when we arrived in Shanghai, and Miss Leaman looking out of the window, cried, "There is Joy-Bell to meet us!" There she stood among the thronging masses. . . . We were expecting Joy-Bell for we had sent a telegram asking her to meet us. What we did not know was that she had not received the wire, but in her morning devotional watch, she had been guided to go down and meet that train. And now our car door stopped at the very spot where she was standing. As we pushed through the frantic crowds, another miracle appeared—two empty taxis waiting at the curb.—**Christiana Tsai,** *Queen of the Dark Chamber*

The Bible is my church. It is always open, and there is my High Priest ever waiting to receive me. There I have my

confessional, my thanksgiving, my psalm of praise . . . and
a congregation of whom the world is not worthy—prophets and apostles, and martyrs and confessors—in short, all
I can want, there I find.—**Charlotte Elliott**

My song shall be of Jesus,
when sitting at his feet,
I call to mind his goodness
and know my joy's complete;
My song shall be of Jesus,
Whatever ills befall,
I'll sing the grace that saves me,
And triumphs over all.
—**Fanny J. Crosby**

Father of mercies, in thy Word what endless glory shines!
For ever be thy name adored for these celestial lines.

Oh, may these heavenly pages be my ever dear delight,
And still new beauties may I see, and still increasing light.

Divine instructor, gracious Lord, be thou for ever near;
Teach me to love thy sacred Word, and find my Savior
  there.
—**Anne Steele**

Mental prayer is nothing else, in my opinion, but friendly
conversation, frequently conversing alone, with One who
we know loves us.—**Teresa of Avila**

I love to steal awhile away from every cumbering care,
And spend the hours of closing day in humble,
    grateful prayer.

I love to think on mercies past, and future good implore,
and all my cares and sorrows cast on God, whom I adore.

I love by faith to take a view of brighter scenes in heaven;
The prospect doth my strength renew, while here by
    tempest driven.

Thus, when life's toilsome day is o'er, may its
    departing ray
Be calm at this impressive hour, and lead to endless day.
—Phoebe H. Brown

Oh, Holy Spirit, come into my heart.
Draw it by thy power to thee, true God,
Grant me love with fear of thee.
Guard me from all evil thought.
Warm me and inflame me with thy love.
Holy my Father and sweet my Lord,
Help me now in all my labors,
Christ who art Love, Christ who art Love.
—Catherine of Siena

My Lord, how full of sweet content,
I pass my years of banishment!
Where'er I dwell, I dwell with thee,
In heaven, in earth, or on the sea.

To me remains nor place nor time:
My country is in every clime:
I can be calm and free from care
On any shore, since God is there.

While place we seek, or place we shun,
The soul finds happiness in none!
But with a God to guide our way,
'Tis equal joy, to go or stay.

Could I be cast where thou art not,
That were indeed a dreadful lot:
But regions none remote I call
Secure of finding God in all.
—**Madame Jeanne Guyon**

My life is one long daily, hourly, record of answered prayer.
—**Mary Slessor**

I believe that we get an answer to our prayers when we
are willing to obey what is implicit in that answer. I believe
that we get a vision of God when we are willing to accept
what that vision does to us.—**Elsie Chamberlain**

My heart rejoices in the LORD;
in the LORD my horn is lifted high. . . .
There is no one holy like the LORD;
there is no one besides you;
there is no Rock like our God.
—**Hannah,** of the Bible, 1 Samuel 2:1-2

When I was young, I could not understand what people meant by "their thoughts wandering in prayer." I asked for what I really wished, and really wished for what I asked. And my thoughts wandered no more than those of a mother would wander, who was supplicating her Sovereign for her son's reprieve from execution.—**Florence Nightingale**

During that time, some amazing changes took place in my heart. The name of Jesus became so precious to me that I could hardly believe it. When I first decided to pray to the supreme God, I had considered Jesus as a Harijan god— the lowest of all gods in rank. Before I knew it, however, I was praying through the name of Jesus. This happened quite unconsciously as a miracle. I was supremely happy, having the assurance that Jesus Christ had suffered for my sin and had forgiven me and blessed me with salvation.
—**B. V. Subbamma,** *New Patterns for Discipling Hindus*

I would like the Angels of Heaven to be amongst us.
I would like the abundance of peace.
I would like full vessels of charity.
I would like rich treasures of mercy.
I would like cheerfulness to preside over all.
I would like Jesus to be present.
—**Brigid of Gael**

O God, whose throne is heaven, whose footstool is the earth below, whose arms enlace the firmament, nothing is hidden from thy sight: in the fastness of the rock thou see'st the diamond, in the bottomless pit of hell, thou see'st thine own just judgment, in the deep recesses of the human heart, thou see'st every secret thought. O God, my Savior, I turn to thee.—**Margaret of Navarre**

O Lord, thou hast set me on high. My flesh is frail and weak. If I therefore at any time forget thee, touch my heart, O Lord, that I may again remember thee. If I swell against thee, pluck me down in my own conceit.—**Queen Elizabeth I**

We are weak: out of weakness make us strong. We are in peril of death: come and heal us. We believe: help thou our unbelief. We hope: let us not be disappointed of our hope. We love: grant us to love much, to love ever more and more, to love all, and most of all to love thee.—**Christina G. Rossetti**

Lord, the day is drawing to a close and, like all the other days, it leaves me with the impression of utter defeat. I have done nothing for thee. . . Yet, O Lord, this sense of deprivation could well be a part of thy divine plan. It could well be that in thine eyes our self-complacency is the most despicable of sins and that we shall come before thy presence in our nakedness that thou, and thou alone, may clothe us.—**Marguerite Teilhard de Chardin**

I am lost, Lord,
I circle and circle,
I do not see for tears,
I feel no direction
and nothing answers my cry—
send me a star.
—**Jo Bingham**

Keep us, Oh God, from pettiness; let us be large in thought, in word, in deed.

Let us be done with fault-finding and leave off self-seeking.

May we put away all pretense and meet each other face to face—without self-pity and without prejudice.

Grant that we may realize that it is the little things that create differences, that in the big things of life we are at one.

And may we strive to touch and to know the great, common heart of us all, and, Oh Lord God, let us forget not to be kind!—**Mary Stewart**

May all your enemies perish,
O Lord!
But may they who love you be like
the sun
when it rises in its strength.
—**Deborah,** of the Bible, Judges 5:31

For this is our Lord's will—that our prayer and our trust be alike, large. Sometimes it cometh to our mind that we have prayed a long time, and yet, seemingly, we have not received an answer. We should not be grieved on this account, but—and I am sure of this in our Lord's meaning—we merely await a better time, a greater grace, or a better gift.—**Julian of Norwich**

I am confounded to think that God, who hath done so much for me, should have so little from me. But this is my comfort, when I come into Heaven, I shall understand perfectly what he hath done for me, and then shall I be able to praise him as I ought.—**Anne Bradstreet**

Make us of quick and tender conscience, O Lord; that understanding we may obey every word of thine, and discerning may follow every suggestion of thine indwelling Spirit.—**Christina G. Rossetti**

O eternal Trinity
Eternal Trinity!
O fire and deep well of charity!
O you who are madly in love
with your creature!
O eternal truth!
O eternal fire!
O eternal wisdom!
Grant us
your gentle and eternal benediction.
Amen.
—**Catherine of Siena**

The knitters of Barracks 28 became the praying heart of the vast diseased body that was Ravensbruck, interceding for all in the camp—guards, under Betsie's prodding, as well as prisoners. We prayed beyond the concrete walls for the healing of Germany, of Europe, of the world.—**Corrie ten Boom,** *The Hiding Place*

Prayer is for us, too, you know. In asking God for help, we are often reminded of how to help ourselves. Paul said we were to "pray without ceasing." He didn't mean, of course, that we were to stop doing everything else. But God created us with the capacity for forming habits. There are good as well as bad ones. Prayer is a creative habit. A way of being.—**Eugenia Price,** *What Really Matters*

Usually when God is going to do a great work, I have noticed that there is a time of great dearth. Nothing moves. Nothing happens. All seems so stagnant. These are golden opportunities for prayer. Our Lord needs prayer, and keeps things from happening, to open space for himself. And he is that satisfying portion we need—that food and drink is himself.—**Joy Ridderhof,** *Mountains Singing*

Sing to the LORD,
for he is highly exalted,
The horse and its rider
he has hurled into the sea.
—**Miriam,** of the Bible, Exodus 15:21

Prayer is the core of our day. Take prayer out, and the day would collapse. . . . But how can you pray—really pray, I mean—with one against whom you have a grudge or whom you have been discussing critically with another? Try it. You will find it cannot be done.—**Amy Carmichael**

There isn't but so much time and the Lord will just have to understand that a mother with little children has to condense her prayers.—**Carie Sydenstricker**

Give your children to God. Give your own self to God. Pray together with your children in honest terms that are appropriate to their age and understanding. Then daily trust God to do his work in all of you.—**Carole Sanderson Streeter,** *Finding Your Place After Divorce*

And his that gentle voice we hear,
Soft as the breath of even,
That checks each fault, that calms each fear,
And speaks of heaven.
—**Harriet Auber**

The whole world is asleep, and God so full of goodness, so great, so worthy of all praise, no one is thinking of him! . . . Nature praises him, and [we] . . . who ought to praise him, sleep!—**Mariam Baouardy**

When sinks the soul subdued by toil to slumber,
Its closing eyes look up to thee in prayer;
Sweet the repose beneath thy wings o'ershading,
but sweeter still to wake and find thee there.

So shall it be at last, in that bright morning
when the soul waketh and life's shadows flee;
O, in that hour, fairer than daylight dawning,
Shall rise the glorious thought—I am with thee.
—**Harriet Beecher Stowe,** "Still, Still with Thee"

Prayer is not eloquence, but earnestness; not the definition
of helplessness, but the feeling of it; not figures of speech,
but earnestness of soul.—**Hannah More**

The glorious armies of the sky
To thee, Almighty King,
Triumphant anthems consecrate,
And hallelujahs sing.

The active lights that shine above,
In their eternal dance,
Reveal their skillful Maker's praise
With silent elegance.
—**Elizabeth Rowe**

Theology

One can never wrestle enough with God if one does so out of pure regard for the truth. Christ likes us to prefer truth to him because, before being Christ, he is truth. If one turns aside from him to go toward the truth, one will not go far before falling into his arms.—**Simone Weil,** *Waiting for God*

Upon that cross of Jesus mine eye at times can see
The very dying form of one who suffered there for me;
And from my smitten heart with tears two wonders
    I confess—
The wonders of redeeming love and my unworthiness.

I take, O cross, thy shadow for my abiding place;
I ask no other sunshine than the sunshine of his face;
Content to let the world go by, to know no gain nor loss,
My sinful self my only shame, my glory all the cross.
—**Elizabeth C. Clephane,** "Beneath the Cross of Jesus"

What I ask of American Christianity is not to show us more creeds, but more of Christ; not more rites and ceremonies, but more religion glowing with love and replete with life,—religion which will be to all weaker races an uplifting power, and not a degrading influence. Jesus Christ has given us a platform of love and duty from which all oppression and selfishness is necessarily excluded.—**Frances Ellen Watkins Harper**

In the same way I could not believe that it was God's ideal will that three-year-old Billy die in such a cruel way. But given a motorized society, given our congested cities, given human free will that resulted in a driver's and a child's carelessness, God would still not suspend the operation of his universe to violate the free will that conspired to bring about this tragedy.—**Catherine Marshall,** *Beyond Our Selves*

A religion that is small enough for our understanding would not be big enough for our needs.—**Corrie ten Boom,** *Clippings from My Notebook*

I'm glad you've figured out free will or whatever. It's great to be able to figure it out but dangerous to put too much faith in your figuring.—**Flannery O'Connor,** *The Habit of Being*

Salvation consists in passing from this dark, restless and tormented Existence in which the worldly man lives, to life in truth, to that in which it is really worth living. This change of spirit becomes possible through experience, the bitter experience that everything is transient. Everything rushes on, everything flies away.—**Catherine of Siena**

When Christians . . . take counsel together, their purpose . . . should not be to ascertain what is the mind of the majority, but what is the mind of the Holy Spirit—something which may be quite different.—**Margaret Hilda Thatcher**

How many of us call the devil by name today? If we see God's love manifested for us in the Incarnation, the life and death and resurrection of Jesus, then we need to also recognize the malignant force that would try to destroy God's love in a particular way, too.—**Madeleine L'Engle,** *Walking on Water*

In all human affairs there are things both certain and doubtful, and both are equally in the hands of God, who is accustomed to guide to a good end the causes that are just and are sought with diligence.—**Isabella, Queen of Spain**

The Spirit within controls the right actions of man. He who has God's grace in his heart cannot go astray.—**Anne Hutchinson**

The only person who does not believe that the Devil is a person is someone who has never attempted to combat him or his ways. . . . The simple tribesman going through his animistic incantations is wiser than such a drugged intellectual. He, at least, knows there is a Devil; and he has ways to appease him temporarily.—**Isobel Kuhn,** *Ascent to the Tribes*

He is not a God far off, but one who may be witnessed and possessed.—**Margaret Fell Fox**

There are three phases of theology; the miraculous, the supernatural, and the "positivist" theology. At first it is quite natural (in an infant state) that infants should think God works by miracles, and should see him in miracles and not in law; then that they should see him in special providence, which is really almost the same as the first; that is the supernatural theology. Lastly, we see him in law. But law is still theology, and the finest.—**Florence Nightingale**

Just as I am, poor, wretched, blind;
Sight, riches, healing of the mind,
Yea, all I need, in thee I find,
O Lamb of God, I come! I come!

Just as I am, thou wilt receive,
Wilt welcome, pardon, cleanse, relieve;
Because thy promise I believe,
O Lamb of God, I come! I come!
—**Charlotte Elliott,** "Just as I Am"

Some of us believe that God is Almighty and may do all, and that he is All-wisdom and can do all; but that he is All-love and will do all—there we stop short.—**Julian of Norwich**

Whatever weakens your reason, impairs the tenderness of your conscience, obscures your sense of God, or takes away the relish of spiritual things; in short, whatever increases the strength and authority of your body over your mind—that thing is sin to you.—**Susanna Wesley**

Let everything be called by its appropriate name, and applied to its proper uses in the sphere to which it belongs. There is a natural and a spiritual love; the natural is first, has its place on the generative plane, and was God-given to subserve useful purposes in that order. But when the spirit calls souls to a higher life—into the resurrection order in the Christ sphere—the natural which was designed to pass away, after having performed its uses, gives place to the higher spiritual love, which infills and permeates the whole being, and is the beginning of eternal life in human souls.—**Antoinette Doolittle**

All true union and harmony of spirit springs from moral conditions and not from those human instincts that we hold in common with the animal creation.—**Martha J. Anderson**

Many are bewailing the low spiritual state of the . . . churches; all of which probably began with a measure of the spirit of grace and truth, but becoming fixed and creed bound, they had no opportunity for spiritual growth. . . . The churches endeavor to derive sustenance from old and time worn theology, and therefore literally starve the people for the lack of a living inspiration and present revelation of light and truth. Why should they not pass away and give place to something better?—**Emily Offord**

Children can be saved! It has often been marvellous in my eyes to recognise the early impress of the Spirit's work.

Even in babes of two and three years of age I have seen that Jesus has made his presence unmistakably realised. —Emma Booth-Tucker

The battle—our battle—against every temptation that can ever try to take us on has already been won on that first Easter morning. All we're involved in is a mopping up operation.—**Dale Evans Rogers,** *God in the Hard Times*

There have been incarnate gods a-plenty, and slain-and-resurrected gods not a few; but [Jesus Christ] is the only God who has a date in history. And plenty of founders of religions have had dates, and some of them have been prophets or avatars of the Divine; but only this one of them was personally God.—**Dorothy L. Sayers,** *The Man Born to be King*

We cannot separate his demands from his love. We cannot dissect Jesus and relate only to the parts that we like or need. Christ died so that we could be forgiven for managing our own lives.—**Rebecca Manley Pippert,** *Out of the Saltshaker and Into the World*

God is, at first, Truth and then Love. But he is only that love which is but one with the sovereign and eternally living truth. In himself, God is love as he is truth.—**Raïssa Maritain**

The Church must . . . not put unbiblical barriers before [people] to make their turning more difficult or impossible. At the same time, she must put clearly before them the biblical conditions for becoming Christians. These barriers the Church is not authorized to remove.
—**B. V. Subbamma,** *New Patterns for Discipling Hindus*

Almighty and Eternal God, the Disposer of all the affairs of the world, there is not one circumstance so great as not to be subject to thy power, nor so small but it comes within thy care.—**Queen Anne**

God holds us accountable for our choices. No one else will answer for you. We can't blame anyone or anything for our choices. People and circumstances influence us, but every day we choose.—**Martha Reapsome,** *The Journey of a Lifetime*

Jesus communicated truth about God or the kingdom of heaven that he wanted his listeners to remember, and so he told them a story. Who could forget how God loves lost people after hearing the stories . . . about the lost sheep, the lost coin, and the lost son? Each tale makes us ask, "Am I like that? Is God like that?"—**Gladys Hunt,** *The Parables of Jesus*

If my religion is true, it will stand up to all my questioning; there is no need to fear. But if it is not true, if it is

man imposing strictures on God (as did the men of the
Christian establishment of Galileo's day) then I want to be
open to God, not to what man says about God. I want to
be open to revelation, to new life, to new birth, to new
light.—**Madeleine L'Engle**, *Walking on Water*

One of the effects of modern liberal Protestantism has been
gradually to turn religion into poetry and therapy, to make
truth vaguer and vaguer and more and more relative, to
banish intellectual distinctions, to depend on feeling instead
of thought, and gradually to come to believe that God has
no power, that he cannot communicate with us, cannot
reveal himself to us, indeed has not done so and that religion
is our own sweet invention.—**Flannery O'Connor,** *The
Habit of Being*

God was executed by people painfully like us, in a society
very similar to our own . . . by a corrupt church, a timid
politician, and a fickle proletariat led by professional
agitators.—**Dorothy L. Sayers,** *The Man Born to Be King*

Did God take his chances
on a son sent to fill flesh?
Was such metamorphosis
a divine risk?
Once embodied
might he not find
earth's poignancies too sharp,
sweet flesh too sweet
to soon discard?

Ah, Father, but you knew
the incarnation was no gamble!
We are the risk you run.
—**Luci Shaw,** *A Widening Light*

The ambition of most Christians . . . is . . . to have a vast
number of things; and their energies are all wasted in
the vain effort to get possession of these things. Some
strive to get possession of certain "experiences;" some
seek after "ecstatic feelings;" some try to make themselves rich in theological "views" and "dogmas"; some
store up a long list of works done and results achieved;
some seek to acquire "illuminations," or to accumulate
"gifts" and "graces." In short, all Christians, almost without exception, seek to possess a store of something or
other, which they fancy will serve to recommend them
to God, and make them worthy of His love and care.
—**Hannah Whitall Smith,** *Every-Day Religion*

It is a profound irony that the Son of God visited this planet
and one of the chief complaints against him was that he
was not religious enough.—**Rebecca Manley Pippert,** *Out
of the Saltshaker and Into the World*

For there are many who study but are ignorant, especially
those who are in spirit arrogant, troubled, and proud, so
eager for new interpretations of the Word (which itself
rejects new interpretations) that merely for the sake of
saying what no one else has said they speak a heresy, and
even then are not content.—**Sor Juana Ines de la Cruz**

The Atheist sure no more can boast aloud
Of chance, or nature, and exclude the God;
As if the clay without the potter's aid
Should rise in various forms, and shapes self-made,
Or worlds above with orb o'er orb profound
Self-mov'd could run the everlasting round.
—**Phillis Wheatley,** "To a Lady on the Death of Three
Relations"

By what
anti-miracle have we
lamed the man
who leaped for joy,
lost ninety-nine
sheep,
turned bread
back to stone
and wine
to water?
—**Luci Shaw,** "Power failure"

Ask the sea if it will ever want water? Do you not know that
the mercies of God are inexhaustible?—**Madame de Combe**

God will take his own time: the business is his.—**Jeanne
Biscot**

One thing that makes me feel a little daffy and which I
hesitate to admit is that I'm inclined to take God entirely

literally. When we make everything symbolic we create distance between ourselves and him and I do think God wants closeness.—**Elizabeth Rooney,** quoted in *Bright Legacy*

Mark this, you that despise and oppose the message of ... God that he sends by women; what had become of the redemption of the whole body of mankind, if they had not cause to believe ... the message that the Lord Jesus sent by these women, of and concerning his resurrection? —**Margaret Fell Fox**

When two truths seem to directly oppose each other, we must not question either, but remember there is a third— God—who reserves to himself the right to harmonize them.—**Madame Anne Soymanov Swetchine**

What can we do to wake the Church up? Too often those who have its destinies in the palm of their hands are chiefly chosen from those who are mere encyclopedias of the past rather than from those who are distinguished by their possession of Divine Power. For leadership of the Church something more is required.—**Catherine Booth**

A tear may often win when every other force fails, and who can say but that what this world of sin and woe most needs, with its cold and indifferent millions, is not so much the courage or the faith or the ability of bygone Christians, but beyond and above all other things the heart made tender, as was even the Lamb of God's, by sanctified suffering.—**Emma Booth-Tucker**

True religion is practical and logical; it takes cognizance of every act, spiritual, intellectual and physical; it teaches us to observe physiological laws as the law of God; that if these are disregarded, suffering and disease will ensue as the just penalty; that they are not imposed upon us by an offended Deity, but are the consequences of violated law. Effect follows cause as sure as night succeeds the day. —**Emily Offord**

We grasp for truth and lose it till it comes to us by love. —**Madeleine L'Engle,** *A Widening Light*

Identity

You are women and a woman is always a beautiful thing. You have been dragged deep in the mud; but still you are women. God calls to you, as He did to Zion long ago, "Awake, awake! Thou that sittest in the dust, put on thy beautiful garments." You can be the friend and companion of Him who came to seek and to save that which was lost. Fractures well healed make us more strong. Take of the very stones over which you have stumbled and fallen, and use them to pave your road to heaven.—**Josephine Butler**

I wish to save up all my charms for heaven; the fashions here do not please me: I hope to be better adorned there than you are now.—**Anne Auverger**

If she have the necessary gifts, and feels herself called by the Spirit to preach, there is not a single word in the whole book of God to restrain her, but many, very many, to urge and encourage her.—**Catherine Booth**

How long shall the fair daughters of Africa be compelled to bury their minds and talents beneath a load of iron pots and kettles? Until union, knowledge and love begin to flow among us. How long shall a mean set of men flatter us with their smiles, and enrich themselves with our hard earnings; their wives' fingers sparkling with rings, and they themselves laughing at our folly? Until we begin to promote and patronize each other. . . . We have never had an opportunity of displaying our talents; therefore the world thinks we know nothing. And we have been possessed of by far too mean and cowardly a disposition. —**Maria Stewart**

For me, this journey toward the truth [toward the "new"] does not demand a rejection of one's past, of one's particular story, of one's particular tradition. No, never that. It is very important to know who you are, and where you have come from—to claim your story.—**Sarah Cunningham,** from *Women of Faith in Dialogue*

I don't know what there is in the word "lady" which will connect itself with all kinds of things I despise and hate; first and most universally it suggests a want of perseverance, and bending before small obstacles, a continual, "I would if. . . ."—**Octavia Hill**

If you are humble, nothing will touch you, neither praise nor disgrace, because you know what you are.—**Mother Teresa**

I have a spiritual suitcase and I know where I'm going. —**Ethel Waters**

At least I do not pretend to have knowledge where I am ignorant. On the contrary, my best claim to indulgence is that I know how much I do not know.—**Hrostwitha**

I was lonely, deadly lonely. And I was to find out then, as I found out so many times, over and over again, that women especially are social beings, who are not content with just husband and family, but must have a community, a group, and exchange with others. ... Young and old, even in the busiest years of our lives, we women especially are victims of the long loneliness. Men may go away and become desert Fathers, but there were no desert mothers.—**Dorothy Day,** *The Long Loneliness*

"A woman is as good as a man" is as meaningless as to say, "a Kaffir is as good as a Frenchman" or "a poet is as good as an engineer" or "an elephant is as good as a racehorse"—it means nothing whatever until you add: "at doing what?"—**Dorothy L. Sayers,** *Are Women Human?*

What dignity can there be in the attitude of women in general, and toward men in particular, when marriage is held (and often necessarily so, being the sole means of maintenance) to be the one end of a woman's life, when it is degraded to the level of a feminine profession, when those who are soliciting a place in this profession resemble the flaccid Brazilian creepers which cannot exist without support, and which sprawl out their limp tendrils in every direction to find something—no matter what—to hang upon; when the insipidity or the material necessities of so many women's lives make them ready to accept almost any man who may offer himself?—**Josephine Butler**

Because I am God's daughter, a bridge, a path, a secret stair
has been built from his heart to mine so that by the Spirit
God's thoughts can step into my mind.—**Luci Shaw,** *God
in the Dark*

My personal perceptions began to shift when I first noticed
in Acts 21:9 that Philip had four daughters who prophesied. I had been taught that prophesy was the highest gift,
the equivalent of today's preaching, and totally a male
prerogative. Yet here were these women who prophesied.
This small verse of Scripture challenged my preconcep-
tions and started me on a new course of study which
continues today.—**Roberta Hestenes,** *Women and Men in
Ministry*

If someone is consumed with climbing the corporate lad-
der, they're out of balance, and it doesn't matter if that
person is married or single, male or female. Choosing a
career that's compatible with a family's particular needs
should be important to men as well as women. Unfortu-
nately, at this stage women are the pioneers in this area,
although a growing number of men are beginning to take
a stand for greater balance in their lives.—**Linda Holland,**
Working Women, Workable Lives

There is much to be unlearned as well as to be learned.
That there is something higher and better in the Christian
religion than rewards and punishments is a new lesson to
thousands of colored people who are still worshiping
under the old dispensation of the slave Bible. But it is not

an easy task to unlearn religious conceptions. "Servants, obey your masters" was preached and enforced by all the cruel instrumentalities of slavery, and by its influence the colored people were made the most valued slaves in the world.—**Fannie Barrier Williams**

No one can make you feel inferior without your consent. —**Eleanor Roosevelt**

I come, not in the strength of steel, but mailed in the panoply of righteousness, to offer my services to my king and country. I ask not the royal signet as a proof of my commission; my credentials are from Heaven. . . . The arm of a woman, in the hands of God to effect a mighty deliverance; will an earthly sovereign refuse her permission to lead his armies?—**Joan of Arc**

O how careful ought we to be, lest through our by-laws of church government and discipline, we bring into disrepute even the word of life. For as unseemly as it may appear now-a-days for a woman to preach, it should be remembered that nothing is impossible with God. And why should it be thought impossible . . . or improper for a woman to preach? seeing the Saviour died for the woman as well as for the man.—**Jarena Lee**

It takes some extra examination to find the numerous women who worked side by side with Paul and the other "well-knowns." Possibly we are slow to notice their names because our own culture has trained us to see women more in strictly family roles than in ministry roles.—**Winnie Christensen,** *Women Who Achieved for God*

Very often, confidence is the single greatest difference between the mediocre and the exceptional, between the joy of service and the pain of it, between looking life in the eye and running from it to hide.—**Maxine Hancock,** *Creative, Confident Children*

One of the first things we learn in our encounter with the Lord is to stop trying to impress him.—**Emilie Griffin,** *Turning*

Man cannot
name himself

He waits for God
or Satan
to tell him
who he is.
—**Luci Shaw,** *The Secret Trees*

If God has no favorites, then the single Christian woman is given complete fulfillment in Jesus Christ as she sits at Jesus' feet and then passes on to others what she has learned. The woman of God needs neither sexual fulfillment nor male protection, neither husband nor children to give her a place in church and society and a sense of identity as a person.—**Kari Torjesen Malcolm,** *Women at the Crossroads*

A man of quality is never threatened by a woman of equality.—**Jill Briscoe,** *Renewal on the Run*

The proof of who we are in Christ isn't how many folks have come to the Lord through us. It isn't how much we've contributed to the Lord's work. It isn't how sweetly we've sung his praises. It is, pure and simple, how we have loved each other.—**Gayle Roper,** *Who Cares?*

As a young woman, I looked into my future and saw freedom from boundaries. I would never have to choose between being traditional or liberated. I could do it all. But instead of assuming I'd be free from all limits, I should have realized that I was being given the freedom to define my own world, to set my own limits. Freedom from boundaries equals disaster. Freedom to establish our own boundaries equals opportunity.—**Karen Scalf Linamen,** *Working Women, Workable Lives*

Oh! my dear mother, you have given me a heart so tender that creatures can never fill it. Let me, then, be the bride of Christ, and of none other.—**Austrebertha**

Do you feel that you just can't survive without a husband?
If so, that's reason enough to make up your mind that
you'll learn how. You can learn to stand up straight by
yourself. You don't have to be in a perpetual leaning position.
But standing up straight means learning to change the way
you think about yourself.—**Carole Sanderson Streeter,**
Finding Your Place After Divorce

Perhaps it is no wonder that the women were first at the
Cradle and last at the Cross. They had never known a man
like this Man—there never has been such another. A
prophet and teacher who never nagged at them, never
flattered or coaxed or patronised; who rebuked without
querulousness and praised without condescension; who
took their questions and arguments seriously; who never
mapped out their sphere for them.—**Dorothy L. Sayers,**
Are Women Human?

Relationships

The family should be the place where each new human being can have an early atmosphere conducive to the development of constructive creativity. Parents, aunts and uncles, grandparents, and sisters and brothers can squash, stamp out, ridicule, and demolish the first attempts at creativity, and continue this demolition long enough to cripple spontaneous outbursts of creation. These things can take place carelessly, and we might be astonished at what we have unconsciously spoiled.—**Edith Schaeffer,** *What Is a Family?*

Jesus, Son of human mother,
Bless our motherhood, we pray;
Give us grace to lead our children,
Draw them to thee day by day;
May our sons and daughters be
dedicated, Lord, to thee.

Thou who didst with Joseph labor,
Nor didst humble work disdain,
Grant we may thy footsteps follow
Patiently through toil or pain;
May our quiet home-life be lived, O Lord, in thee, to thee.
—**Emily L. Shirreff,** "Gracious Savior, Who Didst Honor"

Let my children be committed to thy mercy.—**Katherine von Bora**

My love for you makes me desire your highest good. How can love desire less? Anything that desires less is selfishness, not love. You may have others who will be more demonstrative but never who will love you more unselfishly than your mother or who will be willing to do or bear more for your good.—**Catherine Booth**

When two caring people who are committed to each other wrestle with the inevitable hard times that confront every married couple in a spirit of kindness and tenderness and forgiveness, miracles do happen.—**Dale Evans Rogers,** *God in the Hard Times*

I had an injury when I was a young girl. I was plowing, and the plow hit a root and jumped up and kicked me in the side. The doctor said I wouldn't be able to carry kids. Well, I gave birth to nineteen children. I had two sets of twins. Fifteen of them was born living, and four were stillborn. They were all born at home with a midwife. Today I got twelve of those children, and fifty-four grandchildren, and twenty-seven great-grands. So that doctor, he didn't know nothing, now did he?—**Augusta Jackson,** quoted in *Mothers Talking*

I think it's important to teach our children—as the Bible says—line upon line, precept upon precept, here a little, there a little. If you try to teach a child too rapidly, much will be lost. But the time for teaching and training is preteen. When they reach the teenage years, it's time to shut up and start listening.—**Ruth Bell Graham**

Fathers and mothers, if you have children, they must come first. Your success as a family, our success as a society, depends not on what happens at the White House, but on what happens inside your house.—**Barbara Bush**

Half of the world's sorrows comes from the unwisdom of parents.—**Mary Slessor**

The Bad Mother Who Must Die

She is superior to everyone.
She is omniscient (all knowing)—especially when it comes
   to the feelings and deepest reality of others.
She lives through others.
She has no feelings of her own, but merely
   "shadows" others.
She sees everyone as an extension of herself.
She does not know how to love—only how to control
   (or be controlled).
She is terribly hurt inside, because others have not come
   through for her impossible expectations.
She desperately needs to be needed. She relates to others
   who she fantasizes as "dependent."
She fears not being needed, and thereby rejected.
She can receive something from girls and boys, but not
   from men and women.
—**M. Helene Pollock,** in *Women Ministers*

Children possess an uncanny ability to cut to the core of the issue. . . . One reason for this, I believe, is that children have not mastered our fine art of deception that we call "finesse." Another is that they are so "lately come from God" that faith and trust are second nature to them. They have not acquired the obstructions to faith that come with education.—**Gloria Gaither**

If only God would lean out of heaven and tell me [my children] are going to make it, I could relax. But God doesn't do that. He tells us to be the parents he has called us to be in his strength and promises to do his part. Driven to prayer (after discovering that manipulation didn't work), I began to realize I was only truly positive and confident when I'd been flat on my face before the Lord.—**Jill Briscoe**, *Marriage Matters!*

Our mother-daughter relationships are worthy of all the time and effort that we can devote to them. We will deeply regret doing anything less.—**Elaine McEwan**, *My Mother, My Daughter*

First, does the average good education train our young people in spiritual self-preservation? Does it send them out equipped with the means of living a full and efficient spiritual life? Does it furnish them with a health-giving type of religion; that is, a solid hold on eternal realities, a view of the universe capable of withstanding hostile criticism, of supporting them in times of difficulty and of stress?—**Evelyn Underhill**, *The Life of the Spirit*

The Lord showed me that it's not my place to feel guilty over what my kids are doing, because God is the perfect father and even he has rebellious children. So it can't be solely the parents' responsibility; the children have an accountability of their own.—**Janet,** quoted in *The Lie of the Good Life*

It is in the home that the child learns the basic principle of accountability for actions: first to those around him, and ultimately to God.—**Maxine Hancock,** *Creative, Confident Children*

Do not be sensitive. Perhaps you are by nature, but you can get over it with the exercise of common sense and the help of God. Let things hurt until the tender spot gets callous. Believe that people do not intend to be unkind; some are too busy to think of the feelings of their fellow-workers, and others have not the nice discernment that ought to guide even the busy brain and tongue. Sensitiveness is only another kind of self-consciousness, and as such we should seek deliverance from its irritating power. —**Isabella Thoburn**

Of all the gifts that a parent can give a child, the gift of learning to make good choices is the most valuable and long-lasting.—**Pat Holt & Grace Ketterman,** *Choices Are Not Child's Play*

My husband is not a mother. And that's okay. Because I am.—**Karen Scalf Linamen,** *Working Women, Workable Lives*

This is the irrational season
When love blooms bright and wild.
Had Mary been filled with reason
There'd have been no room for the child.
—**Madeleine L'Engle,** "Annunciation"

What is more deplorable is that mothers otherwise devout ruin themselves by what ought to save them. They fall into [the extreme of] wishing to keep young children in church as long as themselves, which gives them a strong disgust for devotion. This arises from their being surfeited with a food they could not relish, because their stomach was not suited for that nourishment, and for want of power of digestion they conceived such aversion to it that, where it would be suitable for them, they will no longer even try it.—**Madame Jeanne Guyon**

No one faces whiny, weepy, or bright-eyed kids at 3 A.M. because they feel like it. A parent may be desperate, fatigued, angry, helpless, numb, but none is joyful. A child is cared for in the middle of the night for one overriding reason: the child has a need and the parent chooses to meet that need as well as can be done without proper sleep and with the resultant lack of judgment. And this choice to minister is the core definition of biblical love. Biblical love is my choice to act for your good.—**Gayle Roper,** *Who Cares?*

We want more from our mothers than they are ever able to give us, and becoming aware of this pitfall should help us manage the relationships we have with our own daughters.—**Elaine McEwan,** *My Mother, My Daughter*

Son, for mine own part, I have no further delight in anything in this life. What I do here any longer, and to what end I am here, I know not, now that my hopes in this world are accomplished. One thing there was for which I desired to linger for a while in this life—that I might see thee a Catholic Christian before I died. My God hath done this for me, and more; since I now see thee despising earthly happiness, and become his servant: what then do I here? —**Monica,** mother of St. Augustine

How do I love thee? Let me count the ways.
I love thee to the depth and breadth and height
My soul can reach, when feeling out of sight
For the ends of Being and ideal Grace.
I love thee to the level of everyday's
Most quiet need, by sun and candle-light.
I love thee freely, as men strive for Right;
I love thee purely, as they turn from Praise.
I love thee with the passion put to use
In my old griefs, and with my childhood's faith.
I love thee with a love I seemed to lose
With my lost saints,—I love thee with the breath,
Smiles, tears, of all my life!—and, if God choose,
I shall but love thee better after death.
—**Elizabeth Barrett Browning**

I planned my article . . . and then proceeded to write. . . . It was about old maids. "Happy Women" was the title, and I put in my list all the busy, useful, independent spinsters I know, for liberty is a better husband than love to many of us.—**Louisa May Alcott**

I acknowledge the kind hand of the heavenly Father. In changing my name, he has allowed me to take the name of one who loves the cause of Christ, and makes the promotion of it the business of my life. One who is, in every respect, the most calculated to make me happy and useful, of all the persons I have ever seen.—**Ann Hasseltine Judson**

I could not bear the thought of making my dear companion a sharer of the pain [of my crusade for women's legal rights]; yet I saw that we must needs be united in this as in everything else. I had tried to arrange to suffer alone but I could not act alone, if God should indeed call me to action. It seemed to me cruel to have to tell him of the call, and to say to him that I must try and stand in the breach. My heart was shaken by the foreshadowing of what I knew he would suffer.—**Josephine Butler**

The best advice I can give to unmarried girls is to marry someone you don't mind adjusting to.—**Ruth Bell Graham**

It suddenly seemed to me that we had always been near each other, and that we would always be so. Without thinking, I put out my hand and stroked his hair. He looked at me, and all was clear to us. It was one of those tender and peaceful feelings which are like a gift flowing from a region higher than ourselves, illuminating the future and deepening the present. From that moment our understanding was perfect and unchangeable.—**Raïssa Maritain,** *We Have Been Friends Together*

Only in a marriage—a marriage where love is—can sex develop into the delightfully positive force God meant it to be. Here is where the excitement of sex really is. When a man and a woman make a lifelong commitment to love and cherish each other, they are giving themselves the time they will need to dismantly the barriers of restraint, shyness, defensiveness, and selfishness that exist between all human beings. It cannot be done in a night or with a rush of passion. It takes time to know and be known.—**Colleen Townsend Evans,** *A New Joy*

Don't urge me to leave you or to turn back from you. Where you go I will go, and where you stay I will stay. Your people will be my people and your God my God. Where you die I will die, and there I will be buried. May the LORD deal with me, be it ever so severely, if anything but death separates you and me.—**Ruth,** of the Bible, Ruth 1:16-17

Married life . . . isn't a time for settling down but for growth, for doing new things. With each passing year a growing couple will actively look for new and different things they can do together.—**Dale Evans Rogers,** *God in the Hard Times*

The best thing a woman can do for her husband is to make it easy for him to do the will of God.—**Elisabeth Elliot Gren**

We don't naturally grow together and love each other more. We tend to grow apart, to grow distant. So we have to work hard at marriage. It's the most fun work in the world, but still it's work.—**Anne Ortlund**

It is good to have a healthy honesty on the part of those married longer years, as they relate that awful moment of anger when the wedding ring was thrown on the floor and rolled into a crack and took two hours to find and put back on. It is good for the ones married just a short time to know that a marriage can weather "down" moments and rough places, as well as coming to know that it is important to work at relationships. —**Edith Schaeffer,** *What Is a Family?*

Death has sealed off those married years like a capped bottle of perfume. Our marriage cannot be lost or shattered. Nothing can touch it now. It's safe—one of my treasures laid up in heaven where no mothy resentment or rusty dissolution can erode it. In a sense our marriage was like a flower that matured into a fruit, sweet and wholesome, and I am like a seed dropped from that mature fruit, now withered and dead. I am the result of a long relationship and I want to fall in good ground and produce more fruit—of what kind God and I will have to determine. —**Luci Shaw,** *God in the Dark*

The whole submission issue is so far down on the list of [my husband's] and my priorities that we don't think about it at all anymore. It's so much more important to figure out how to be a Christian, how to live the Christian life—submission is a minor issue in comparison.—**Wendy,** quoted in *The Lie of the Good Life*

How many lives are marred and made miserable by the selfishness of some relative or friend (too often, alas! a parent), who, under the plea of exceeding love, will not allow the least liberty of action in the loved ones, and will do everything possible to hinder their development in every line that does not conduce to their own personal pleasure, or is not agreeable to themselves. Surely such a course, however it may be disguised, can spring from nothing but pure unadulterated selfishness. The law of love can never be a cherishing of self at the expense of the loved one, but must always be the cherishing of the loved one at the expense of self.—**Hannah Whitall Smith,** *Every-Day Religion*

I was angry because I cared. If I hadn't loved them, I could have walked away. But love detests what destroys the beloved. Real love stands against the deception, the lie, the sin that destroys.—**Rebecca Manley Pippert,** *Hope Has Its Reasons*

Success in marriage depends on being able when you get over being in love, to really love. . . . You never know anyone until you marry them.—**Eleanor Roosevelt,** *My Day*

Yes, marriage is a great risk—it's a plunge into the deep. But the greater the risk we take on God, the deeper and farther we dare to go from the safe shore, the richer shall be the treasures we will find and the greater the delights. —**Ingrid Trobisch,** *On Our Way Rejoicing!*

Lord, I am not worthy of so good a husband; but help us both to observe the holiness of wedded life, so that we may eternally abide together near thee.—**Elizabeth of Hungary**

Your home can be a place for dying or living, for wilting or blooming, for anxiety or peace, for discouragement or affirmation, for criticism or approval, for profane disregard or reverence, for suspicion or trust, for blame or forgiveness, for alienation or closeness, for violation or respect, for carelessness or caring. By your daily choices, you will make your home what you want it to be.—**Carole Sanderson Streeter,** *Finding Your Place After Divorce*

Make no mistake about it, responsibilities toward other human beings are the greatest blessings God can send us.—**Dorothy Dix**

[Love] is the divine vitality that everywhere produces and restores life. To each and every one of us, it gives the power of working miracles if we will.—**Lydia Maria Child**

When trying to understand God's purposes for our families, we often limit ourselves to those passages that relate specifically to husbands, wives, and children. In so doing, it is easy to overlook the fact that all of the instruction given to Christians in general can well be applied to Christians who are living together in families!—**R. Ruth Barton,** *Becoming Women of Purpose*

Our families can survive with less of what we do. They just can't get by with less of what we give them out of who we are. Maybe we can't "do it all." But we can still give our families our hearts. We can turn our houses into homes, our families into, well, families. And one of the ways we can do it is by cherishing, not relegating, our special place as women, wives, and mothers in our homes. —**Karen Scalf Linamen,** *Working Women, Workable Lives*

If ever two were one, then surely we.
If ever man were lov'd by wife, then thee;
If ever wife was happy in a man,
Compare me with ye women if you can.
I prize thy love more than whole mines of gold,
Or all the riches that the East doth hold.
My love is such that rivers cannot quench,

Nor aught but love from thee, give recompense.
Thy love is such I can no way repay,
The heavens reward thee manifold, I pray.
Then while we live, in love let's so persever
That, when we live no more, we may live ever.
—**Anne Bradstreet,** "To my dear and loving husband"

We can have no relationship of depth or authenticity if we insist there is nothing wrong with us, or that it is always the other person's fault. . . . To refuse to take responsibility and admit our flaws makes the intimacy and love we seek in relationships an impossibility.—**Rebecca Manley Pippert,** *Hope Has Its Reasons*

Our kids face such criticism and so many closed doors in the mere act of being alive that we as parents need to encourage them all we can.—**Gayle Roper,** *Who Cares?*

Life Seasons
and
Changes

In youth we learn; in age we understand.—**Marie Ebner-Eschenbach**

The springtime was past, and we were approaching the end of the warm summer days of child rearing. Now autumn love, weighted with its rich colors of the changing season, waited for us. It would be different, but it would be rich in a variety of ways as surely as autumn was different from spring. This lesson, however, didn't save me from any of the natural pain as the process began to take place. No tree likes to lose its leaves.—**Jill Briscoe,** *Marriage Matters!*

Parting after parting
All one's life long;
It's a bitter pang, parting
While love and life are strong.

Parting after parting
Sore fear and sore sore pain
Till one dreads the pang of meeting
More than of parting again.
—**Christina G. Rossetti**

I look back on my life like a good day's work.—**Grandma Moses**

Our lives are never more profoundly touched or inalterably changed than at the place of suffering. It is an experience we cannot escape. Yet often we attempt to turn our eyes away from rather than toward other people's suffering.—**Brita Gill,** in *Women Ministers*

Thou, O Lord, hast freed us from the fear of death. Thou hast made the end of this life the beginning to us of true life. . . . One day thou wilt take again what thou hast given, transfiguring with immortality and gracing our mortal remains. Thou hast saved us from the curse and from sin, having become both for our sake.—**Macrina**

Thou knowest, O God, that I would set his presence—most delightful to me—before all the joys and enchantments of this world, had thy graciousness yielded him to me. But now I lay at thy disposal him and me, as thou wilt. Nay, though I could call him back at the cost of the smallest hair of my head, I would not call him back against thy will.—**Elizabeth of Hungary,** after her husband's death

God is the same when he afflicts as when he is merciful, just as worthy of our entire trust and confidence.—**Ann Hasseltine Judson**

The coffin of every hope is the cradle of a good experience.—**Florence Nightingale**

In every deed there is a fellowship of suffering. Our modern way of looking upon suffering as a thing which by good arrangement, we can get rid of, misses often that solemn sense of its holiness, which those who live in constant memory of our Lord's suffering, enter into. —Octavia Hill

I do not want to die without leaving a record of my belief that suffering can be overcome. For I do believe it. What must one do? One must submit. Do not resist. Take it. Be overwhelmed. Accept it fully. Make it part of life. Everything in life that we really accept undergoes a change. —**Katherine Mansfield,** from *Letters of Katherine Mansfield to John Middleton Murry*

And when I mourn I am filled with pain that seems unbearable at first. . . . Sometimes it turns to tears, and sometimes to quiet moments of reflection. It doesn't matter which. The important thing is that I am made vulnerable, receptive—to more pain? Perhaps, but certainly to God's healing love. And Jesus, who knew the human longing for a departed friend, makes the pain bearable and the loss understandable.—**Colleen Townsend Evans,** *A New Joy*

It is how you open your life to pain. what you let Jesus do with it. it is becoming friends with pain. . . . walking beside her . . . embracing her. many of our greatest surprises have come from pain and suffering.—**Ann Kiemel Anderson,** *First Love*

How necessary it is for young people . . . to lay down a plan for our conduct in life in order to live not only agreeably in this early season of it, but with cheerfulness in maturity, comfort in old age, and with happiness to Eternity; and I can find but one scheme to attain all these desirable ends and that is the [Christian] scheme. To live agreeably to the dictates of reason and religion, to keep a strict guard over not only our actions but our very thoughts before they ripen into action, to be active in every good word and work must produce a peace and calmness of mind beyond expression.—**Eliza Lucas Pinckney**

In admitting that my father had died . . . I was discovering that saying good-by to a loved one who has died is not the same as forgetting them or ceasing to think of them. It is simply the way of owning the loss, integrating it, accepting its restrictions and limitations and saying yes to life without the one who has died.—**Joyce Huggett,** *Listening to Others*

I think that the dying pray at the last not "please," but "thank you," as a guest thanks his host at the door. Falling from airplanes the people are crying thank you, thank you, all down the air; and the cold carriages draw up for them on the rocks. Divinity is not playful. The universe was not made in jest but in solemn incomprehensible earnest. By a power that is unfathomably secret, and holy, and fleet. There is nothing to be done about it, but ignore it, or see.—**Annie Dillard,** *Pilgrim at Tinker Creek*

There is grief that is useful, and there is grief that is destructive. The first sort consists in weeping over one's own faults and weeping over the weakness of one's neighbours, in order not to destroy one's purpose, and attach oneself to the perfect good. But there is also grief that comes from the enemy, full of mockery, which some call accidie. This spirit must be cast out, mainly by prayer and psalmody.—**Mother Syncletica**

After [I learned that my husband had expired] I remained in a very great silence, exterior and interior; silence, however, dry and without support. I could neither weep nor speak. My mother-in-law said very beautiful things, at which everyone was edified, and they were scandalized at my silence, which was put down to want of resignation. A monk told me that everyone admired the beautiful behavior of my mother-in-law; that as for me, they did not hear me say anything—that I must offer my loss to God. But it was impossible for me to say a single word, whatever effort I made. I was, besides, much prostrated, for although I had recently given birth to my daughter, I nevertheless watched my husband without leaving his room the twenty-four nights he was ill. I was more than a year in recovering from the fatigue of that.—**Madame Jeanne Guyon**

Many times in my life in practical affairs I have had my "mourning turned into dancing," because I have found that the trial I mourned was really a gateway into the good things I longed for. And I cannot help suspecting that this is far more often the case than we are inclined to think. —**Hannah Whitall Smith,** *Every-Day Religion*

My son, my son Symphorian, remember the living God, and be of good cheer. Raise thy heart to heaven, and think of him that reigneth there. Fear not death which leads to certain life.—**Mother of Symphorian**

I have lost all! Oh, my beloved brother—oh, the friend of my heart—oh, my good and pious husband, thou art dead, and hast left me in misery! How shall I live without thee? Ah, poor lonely widow and miserable woman that I am; may he who forsakes not widows and orphans console me. Oh! my God, console me! Oh! my Jesus, strengthen me in my weakness.—**Elizabeth of Hungary**

Go, my child, confide in God; for angels will bear thee, like Lazarus, to the place of thy rest.—**Madame de Chantal**

A wife at daybreak I shall be,
Sunrise, thou hast a flag for me?
At midnight I am yet a maid—
How short it takes to make it bride!
Then, Midnight, I have passed from thee
Unto the East and Victory.

Midnight, "Good night"
I hear thee call.
The angels bustle in the hall,
Softly my Future climbs the stair,
I fumble at my childhood's prayer—
So soon to be a child no more!
Eternity, I'm coming, sir—
Master, I've seen that face before.
—**Emily Dickinson,** "Eternity, I'm coming"

Though man is born to trouble, yet I believe there is scarce a man to be found upon earth but, take the whole course of his life, hath more mercies than afflictions, and much more pleasure than pain.—**Susanna Wesley**

I am well. All is well, well forever. I see, wherever I turn my eyes, whether I live or die, nothing but victory.... I am as conscious of the presence of God as I am of the presence of those I have with me.—**Lady Huntingdon**

We must never get into the habit of being preoccupied with the future. There is no reason to do so. God is there.
—**Mother Teresa,** *Total Surrender*

I am really eager to have another generation in the house. In fact, I think if I had my life to live over, I would try to locate my family closer to grandparents. . . . If you are involved intimately with someone who is aging, and you have a positive relationship, it's a lesson. It teaches you that growing old is perhaps something that isn't so terrible or frightening.—**Mary,** quoted in *Mothers Talking*

It's so important to live fully. Since grief is my assignment for today, Lord, help me to grieve wholeheartedly, allowing the reality of the grief to possess me until it becomes appropriate to move beyond it.—**Elizabeth Rooney,** in *Bright Legacy*

On my way back I met a little girl with a pitcher in her hand. We both stopped, and with the instinctive, unconventional camaraderie of childhood plunged into an intimate, confidential conversation. She was a jolly little soul, with black eyes and two long braids of black hair. We told each other how old we were, and how many dolls we had, and almost everything else there was to tell except our names which neither of us thought about. When we parted, I felt as though I were leaving a life long friend. We never met again.—**Lucy Maud Montgomery,** *The Alpine Path*

I would do nothing differently regarding choices I've made—my training, career, life partner, having children, the mission work, our lifestyle. Obviously I wish I'd done it all better. I do wish I would have worried less about all those things.—**Jill Briscoe**

At the end of your life, you will never regret not having passed one more test, not winning one more verdict or not closing one more deal. You will regret time not spent with a husband, a friend, a child or a parent.—**Barbara Bush**

Life goes on. Nobody who is truly alive is looking back at a finished story. At best, some are able to see that certain chapters of their lives have come to a close, and can offer the wisdom of perspective.—**Alice Slaikeu Lawhead,** *The Lie of the Good Life*

There is something satisfying, rejuvenating, comforting about the seasons of a year—and the seasons of womanhood. The seasons remind me that I play one small part in a bigger picture—that there is a pulse, a sequence, a journey set into motion by the very hand of God himself. The seasons remind me daily of God's timing, of nature, of the ebb and flow of life, of the things that matter.—**Karen Scalf Linamen,** *Working Women, Workable Lives*

My darling firstborn child thou hast pleased to take from me; and as thy wisdom saw fit not [to] accept him as servant, I thank thee that thou art pleased to accept him as a saint, spotless and innocent as I received him from thee. Oh that he may be as acceptable an offering as Abraham's only son in thy sight!—**Margaret Hill Morris**

Death is the opening of a more subtle life. In the flower, it sets free the perfume; in the chrysalis, the butterfly; in man, the soul.—**Juliette Adam**

When I buried my husband, I buried all my earthly love with him, for though I loved him as my own soul, I would not for a penny buy back his life against the will of God. . . . [N]ow my soul will love God only.—**Bridget of Sweden**

Suddenly there was the feeling of being surrounded by the love of God the Father—enveloped in it, cradled with infinite gentleness. . . .

Much later . . . I realized that God had given me this experience in the hours preceding Peter's death so that I might have absolute assurance that he was beside Peter and me every minute, loving us, sharing Peter's glory and my grief.—**Catherine Marshall,** *Beyond Our Selves*

Neither life nor death shall ever
From the Lord his children sever;
Unto them his grace he showeth,
And their sorrows all he knoweth.

Though he giveth or he taketh,
God his children ne'er forsaketh;
His the loving purpose solely
To preserve them pure and holy.
—**Carolina Sandell Berg,** "Children of the Heavenly Father"

Clouds may gather over our home in times of sickness or bereavement; but the influence of a sweet Christian character shines through the clouds with a golden radiance, brings a lasting blessing to those who remain.—**Christiana Tsai,** *Queen of the Dark Chamber*

Nothing is far to God; nor need I fear lest he should be ignorant at the end of the world of the place when he is to raise me up.—**Monica,** mother of Augustine

Life
Work

Work is the natural exercise and function of man. . . . Work is not primarily a thing one does to live, but the thing one lives to do. It is, or should be, the full expression of the worker's faculties, the thing in which he finds spiritual, mental and bodily satisfaction, and the medium in which he offers himself to God.—**Dorothy L. Sayers**

We have found sickness and poverty to relieve, widows to protect, advice to be given in every possible difficulty or emergency, teachers and Bible women to be trained, houses to be built, horses and cattle to be bought, gardens to be planted, and accounts to be kept and rendered. We have found use for every faculty, natural and acquired, that we possessed, and have coveted all that we lacked.—**Isabella Thoburn**

I think that we both have high views of the Art we follow, and steadfast purpose in the pursuit of it, and that we should not, either of us, be likely to be thrown from the course, by the casting of any Atalanta-ball of speedy popularity.—**Elizabeth Barrett Browning**

I believe my King suggests a thought, and whispers me a musical line or two, and then I look up and thank him delightedly and go on with it. That is how my hymns come.—**Frances Ridley Havergal**

Painting, better than any other means, enables us to see the humility of the saints, the constancy of the martyrs, the purity of the virgins, the beauty of the angels, the love and charity with which the seraphim burns. It raises and transports mind and soul beyond the stars, and leaves us to contemplate the eternal sovereignty of God.—**Vittoria Colonna**

It is the only way to keep money, or land, or talent, or happiness—give it away. If only every one had studied the divine arithmetic, what a world it would be.—**Helen Barrett Montgomery**

One star differs from another in glory, yet all shine; so one organization comprehends more of the Divine than another; yet all truths are of God. The agitation of thought develops mind. A rap on the head set Newton to thinking. So prone is the human mind to the narrowness of educational prejudices that it often requires severe raps to break the old shell of conservatism and let in the new light of progressive truths.—**Marcia M. Bullard**

Treasure up the gifts of God; the time will come when you will need them; and if you are faithful to treasure up the gifts of God, then they will wake up in your soul.—**a Shaker mother**

That my natural gifts might not be made void by negligence I have been at pains, whenever I have been able to

pick up some threads and scraps torn from the old mantle
of philosophy, to weave them into the stuff of my own
book.—**Hrostwitha**

Now, almighty God, I pray, receive this holy song
and unloose the lips of your everlasting, sevenfold spirit
and open the inner-most sanctuaries of my heart
so that I, Proba the seer, may reveal all the sacred
    mysteries. . . .
I shall begin now to hymn the libations of holy light
which in my thirst I have drunk. Be present, O God,
    and guide my mind.
May I tell how Vergil sang of Christ's holy gifts.
I shall make this story clear to all, commencing at the very
    beginning. . . .
For, Yes, I confess, I used to sing of trivial spectacles;
always I sang of horses and arms, of heroes and battles.
With zeal for vain labor did I ply my craft.
As I tried everything a greater will seemed
to reveal truths buried deep in earth and fog.
Day after day my mind stirred, eager to try
something great, content with neither peace nor rest.
—**Proba**

And who among us has not proved that however stammer-
ing the utterance, or feeble the capacity, the unwaxed, untu-
tored, childlike outpourings of the new convert's first love
wields an influence far beyond that of the most polished
or eloquent discourse. In a thousand different ways, the
indefinable touch of simplicity conquers when the com-
bined forces of might utterly fail.—**Emma Booth-Tucker**

There is but one Christ, who is the Sun of righteousness, in the midst of an innumerable company of Saints and Angels; those Saints have their degrees even in this life, some are stars of the first magnitude, and some of a lesser degree; and others (and they indeed the most in number), but small and obscure, yet all receive their luster (be it more or less) from that glorious sun that inlightens all in all; and, if some of them shine so bright while they move on earth, how transcendently splendid shall they be, when they are fixed in their heavenly spheres!—**Anne Bradstreet**

Humorously enough, it has been men who have set me free to exercise gifts some other men say I shouldn't have! When men debate "my gift" nowadays, I ask them to be gentle with me and instead of saying "women can or cannot do this or that," to try putting my name in there and say instead, "Jill can or cannot do this or that." Those who know and love me find that difficult to do! Gifts, I have discovered, are not gendered.—**Jill Briscoe,** *Marriage Matters!*

Making grace believable to the contemporary reader is the almost insurmountable problem of the novelist who writes from the standpoint of Christian orthodoxy.—**Flannery O'Connor**

I have done what I could.—**Carry Nation**

Vision is of God. A vision comes in advance of any task well done.—**Katherine Logan**

I felt that my vocation imposes upon me the necessity of remaining outside the church, without so much as engaging myself in any way, even implicly, to her or to the dogmas of Christianity . . . in order that I may serve God and the Christian faith in the realm of intelligence.—**Simone Weil,** *Waiting for God*

Sometimes it is hard to admit that overwork is a sin, but it is. Overwork is destructive of the temple of the Holy Spirit. It dims the vision, sharpens the temper, kills creativity, and deadens spiritual sensitivity.—**M. Helene Pollock**

While alone on my knees one Sabbath . . . as I lifted my heart to God crying, "What wouldst thou have me to do?" there was borne in my mind, as I believe from loftier regions, this declaration, "You are to speak for woman's ballot as a weapon for protection for her home." Then for the first and only time in my life, there flashed through my brain a complete line of arguments and illustrations. —**Frances Willard**

Christ moves among the pots and pans.—**Teresa of Avila**

Life is a hard fight, a struggle, a wrestling with the Principle of Evil, hand to hand, foot to foot. Every inch of the way must be disputed. The night is given us to take breath, to pray, to drink deep at the fountain of power. The day, to use the strength which has been given us, to go forth to work with it till the evening.—**Florence Nightingale**

Today we stand on the threshold of woman's era, and woman's work is grandly constructive. In her hand are possibilities whose use or abuse must tell upon the political life of the nation, and send their influence for good or evil across the track of unborn ages. . . . Men may boast of the aristocracy of blood, may glory in the aristocracy of talent, and be proud of the aristocracy of wealth, but there is one aristocracy which must ever outrank them all, and that is the aristocracy of character; and it is the women of a country who help to mold its character, and to influence if not determine its destiny.—**Frances Ellen Watkins Harper**

A certain young man came to Mother with some peach and plum stones in his hand, and asked her if he might plant them? "Yes," answered Mother, "do all your work as though you had a thousand years to live, and as you would if you knew you must die to-morrow."—**Lucy Wright**

Every cycle has its prophets—as guiding stars; and they are the burning candles of the Lord to light the spiritual temple on earth, for the time being. When they have done their work, they will pass away; but the candlesticks will remain, and other lights will be placed in them. —**Antoinette Doolittle**

Several ministers whom I had never seen before told me, at different times, that God was calling me to the ministry, and that I would have to go. I said, "If I were a man I would love to work for Jesus." They told me I had a work to do which no man could do; the Lord was calling me to the West to labor for lost souls. I said, "O Lord! I cannot take Willie with me, nor can I leave him behind." Then the Lord saw fit to take him out of the way; so he laid his hand on my darling little boy, and in a few days took him home to heaven. He was the joy of my life. He was nearly seven years old. He was very bright for one of his age—in fact, far beyond his years. . . . He bid us all good-bye and said he was going to be with Jesus. He died very happy. . . . The dear Savior was never so near and real to me before. He was by my side and seemed to bear me up in his loving arms. I could say, "The Lord gave and the Lord has taken away; blessed be the name of the Lord."—**Maria Woodworth-Etter**

Were it not for God's grace I could do nothing. Had I not the assurance that God directs my work, I would rather tend sheep than expose myself to such great perils.—**Joan of Arc**

It is so much better just to be able to say, "Send me" without having to add "where I shall have my position properly recognized, or opportunities to use my special gifts." It is God whom we want to get recognized, not us.—**Evelyn Underhill,** *Mixed Pasture*

I cannot remember the time when I was not writing, or when I did not mean to be an author. To write has always been my central purpose around which every effort and hope and ambition of my life has grouped itself. I was an indefatigable little scribbler, and stacks of manuscripts, long ago reduced to ashes, alas, bore testimony to the same. I wrote about all the little incidents of my existence. I wrote descriptions of my favourite haunts, biographies of my many cats, histories of visits, and school affairs, and even critical reviews of the books I had read.—**Lucy Maud Montgomery**

You cannot make your decisions based on criticisms. You have to do what you think is right.—**Rosalynn Carter**

The artist is a servant who is willing to be a birthgiver. In a very real sense the artist (male or female) should be like Mary who, when the angel told her that she was to bear the Messiah, was obedient to the command. Obedience is an unpopular word nowadays, but the artist must be obedient to the work, whether it be a symphony, a painting, or a story for a small child. I believe that each work of art, whether it is a work of great genius, or something very small, comes to the artist and says, "Here I am. Enflesh me. Give birth to me."—**Madeleine L'Engle,** *Walking on Water*

I felt at times that I must exercise in the ministry, but when I rose upon my feet I felt ashamed, and so I went under a cloud for some time, and endeavored to keep silence; but I could not quench the Spirit. I was rejected by the elders and rulers. . . . I was hunted down in every place where I appointed a meeting. . . . I persevered, notwithstanding the opposition of those who were looked upon as higher

and wiser. . . . I arose, and after expressing a few words,
the Spirit came upon me with life, and a victory was
gained over the power of darkness, and we could rejoice together in his love.—**Elizabeth,** African slave and
minister

I listen to my stories; they are given to me, but they don't
come without a price. We do have to pay, with hours of
work that ends up in the wastepaper basket, with in-
tense loneliness, with a vulnerability that often causes
us to be hurt. And I'm not sure that it's a choice. If we're
given a gift—and the size of the gift, small or great, does
not matter—then we are required to serve it, like it or
not, ready or not.—**Madeleine L'Engle,** *The Rock That Is
Higher*

Can we wonder at the mortal weariness and disgust, the
sense of wasted powers and the conviction that her life is
a failure, that comes over a woman when, instead of the
ever-broadening activities she had planned, she finds herself tied down to the petty work to teaching a few girls.
—**Lottie Moon**

Send whom thou wilt to kings and rulers of the earth, but
let me be a servant to the servants of my Lord. Let me
administer to the afflicted members of my exalted and
glorious Redeemer. Let this be my lot, and I give the glories
of the world to the wind.—**Elizabeth Rowe**

My mind is absorbed with the sufferings of man. Since I was twenty-four there never [has been] any vagueness in my plans or ideas as to what God's work was for me.
—**Florence Nightingale**

Not the great and gifted only
He appoints to do his will,
But each one, however lowly,
Has a mission to fulfill.

Knowing this, toil we unwearied,
With true hearts and purpose high;
We would win a wreath immortal
Whose bright flowers ne'er fade and die.
—**Charlotte Forten**

I can imagine an easier life, but with love, health, and work I can be happy; for these three help one to do, to be, and to endure all things.—**Louisa May Alcott**

My children, be encouraged in this work; you are in the bond of the covenant—although you may be breakers of covenant, yet God is merciful keeper of covenant. Endeavor as you grow up, to own and renew your covenant, and rest not if God give you life, but so labor to improve all the advantages that God is pleased to afford you, that you may be fit to enjoy the Lord Jesus Christ in all his ordinances.—**Sarah Goodhue**

Ministry
and
Service

If God has called you, do not spend time looking over your shoulder to see who is following.—**Corrie ten Boom,** *Clippings from My Notebook*

I was free; but there was no one to welcome me to the land of freedom. I was a stranger in a strange land, and my home after all was down in the old cabin quarter, with the old folks, and my brothers and sisters. But to this solemn resolution I came; I was free, and they should be free also; I would make a home for them in the North, and the Lord helping me, I would bring them all there. Oh, how I prayed then, lying all alone on the cold, damp ground: "Oh, dear Lord," I said, "I ain't got no friend but you. Come to my help, Lord, for I'm in trouble!"—**Harriet Tubman**

The biggest disease today is not leprosy or tuberculosis, but rather the feeling of being unwanted, uncared for and deserted by everybody. The greatest evil is the lack of love and charity.—**Mother Teresa**

A soul cannot live without loving. It must have something to love for it was created in love.—**Catherine of Siena**

It seems too adventurous perhaps, but God is able. I have no one save the Holy Ghost to rely upon. My weak health and lack of ability seem to deny me success, but when I

am weak, God is strong. Depending upon him alone, I go forward to establish the Sanatorium. To be with the children makes me happy and perhaps some will call me neglectful of my duty as a mother. But though my eyes are wet with tears, I must go forward. O Lord, fill me with the Holy Ghost. Give me power to move the people. Amen.
—**Kiye Sato Yamamuro**

My stay in the Congo has been a time of passionate, incessant, satisfying activity. Sometimes I have thought that the loveliest thing that could happen would be to bleed to death out of pure love for Africa. As long as one loves, one lives nobly. Helping others to climb one grows in stature. That is why a fire burns within me. If my inner life dries up, all my missionary work becomes soulless. . . becomes just an eccentric way of life. But it is easier to walk on the edge of a knifeblade than to live out integral Christianity here.—**Ruth Siegfried**

Who can estimate the results of missionary service in China? It made Christ known; it built churches, schools, orphanages and hospitals far and wide; it opened the door for women to enter the schools and have the same opportunities as men; it helped rouse the people to the evils of foot-binding for women, and opium-smoking; it healed the sick . . . fed famine victims, and cared for the war sufferers . . . it showed the infinite value of a human soul in God's eyes, and wherever the light of the gospel shone, it enlightened that society.—**Christiana Tsai,** *Queen of the Dark Chamber*

We have learned in these days of change and confrontation that we cannot love everyone's ideas, but we are committed to love one another. And that will, please God, carry us through.—**Ann Patrick Ware,** from *Women of Faith in Dialogue*

Ever since the day I received the grace of vocation from our Lord through his servant Francis, no suffering hath ever troubled me, no penance too hard, no infirmity too great.—**Clare of Assisi**

Those who rule must above all be able to rule themselves.—**Catherine of Siena**

Be brave and dare with a holy boldness.—**Teresa of Avila**

Help me, Lord, to remember that religion is not to be confined to the church or closet, nor exercised only in prayer and meditation, but that everywhere I am in thy Presence.—**Susanna Wesley**

O Lord, may I be directed what to do and what to leave undone.—**Elizabeth Fry**

God grant us faith and courage to keep "hands off" and allow the new garden of the Lord's planting to ripen.
—**Lottie Moon**

O God, Thou puttest into my heart this great desire to devote myself to the sick and sorrowful. I offer it to thee. Give me my work to do.—**Florence Nightingale**

Christ was never in a hurry. There was no rushing forward, no anticipating, no fretting over what might be. Each day's duties were done as every day brought them, and the rest was left with God.—**Mary Slessor**

I am growing more and more anxious that my life may be given without reserve to God's service. If we start out with the purpose of always doing the very highest thing we know, we must have a great deal of courage and honest conviction, for it would often be a hard thing to choose. —**Helen Barrett Montgomery**

Lord, if being a martyr for thee would glorify thee, all right; just to go down there and be butchered by wicked men for their own gratification, without any reference to thy glory, I'm not willing.—**Amanda Smith**

In this day, when all the tendency is towards conventionality, and towards a stereotyped appearance rather than a reality, how beautiful, how powerful, how essential as an implement of Gospel service is the simple sincerity of the little child!—**Emma Booth-Tucker**

I was looking on, not knowing what to do, [and] the Spirit of God brought before me the vision I had before I started out in the work of the Lord, and said: "Don't you remember when you were carried away, and saw the field of wheat and the sheaves falling? The large field of wheat was the multitudes of people you are to preach the gospel to; the falling sheaves is what you see here tonight, the slaying power of God. This is my power; I told you I would be with you and fight your battles; it is not the wisdom of men, but the power and wisdom of God that is needed to bring sinners from darkness to light." The Lord revealed wonderful things to me in a few moments: my fears were all gone.—**Maria Woodworth-Etter**

Firm and steadfast in good works
Make me, and in thy service
Make to persevere,

So that I may be able always
To please thee,
Lord Jesus Christ.
—Clare of Assisi

When it becomes clear to me that I am to play a major role in this person's life, like offering counseling or prayer ministry over a period of time . . . I try to insure that I am supported in four ways—by a group of people who are holding on to me and the entire situation in prayer, by

supervision from someone more skilled . . . than I am, by
the assent and love of my husband, and by insuring that I
take sufficient time for rest and relaxation and personal
prayer.—**Joyce Huggett,** *Listening to Others*

Let me never give way to the trouble and restlessness of
an unquiet mind, which grows weary and slackens in the
duties of its state, envying the fancied happiness of other
conditions of life.—**Madame de Maintenon**

Another year is dawning,
Dear Father, let it be,
In working or in waiting,
Another year with thee;
Another year of progress,
Another year of praise,
Another year of proving
Thy presence all the days.
—**Frances Ridley Havergal**

There is a time for sowing. No anticipation of harvest
advantages, no assurance of its sunlit splendour or its
golden riches can make us independent of its arduous toil
and the out-of-sight sacrifice of the weary sowing season.—**Emma Booth-Tucker**

Help us, O God, to do our best to help other people to
accomplish and to achieve, knowing that their contribution
is what God is trying to give the world.—**Florence Simms**

We send up a cry of thanksgiving for people of all races, creeds, classes and colors the world over, and pray that through the instrumentality of our lives the spirit of peace, joy, fellowship and brotherhood shall circle the world.
—**Mary McLeod Bethune**

Those who say there is nothing sacred have never fed hungry children. They have not heard the whisking wires beating circles in the boiling water and foaming milk. They have never heard the laughter of the workers, or seen the children pressing in line, seven hundred of them waiting to drink. They have not placed cups of milk, warm and sweet, at the railing. They do not know that whatever increases the humanity of another is a holy act, and whatever decreases it is unholy.—**Karen Burton Mains,** *The Fragile Curtain*

I have gotten at different times in my life extraodinarily much more out of [service projects] than I've given.
—**Barbara Bush**

A disturber of the peace am I? Yes indeed, of my own peace. Do you call this disturbing the peace that instead of spending my time in frivolous amusements I have visited the plague infested and carried out the dead? I have visited those in prison and under sentence of death. Often for three days and three nights I have neither eaten nor slept. I have never mounted the pulpit, but I have done more than any minister in visiting those in misery. Is this disturbing the peace of the church?—**Katherine Zell**

Any number of factors can make us feel limited or inadequate: lack of education or Christian upbringing, a physical handicap, our marital status (singleness, divorce, marriage to an unsaved spouse), financial limitations, young children in the home, or even the way we view our bodies or our personalities. However, these are only perceived limitations. So often, what we see as limitations are God's training ground for unique ministry and a showcase for his strength and glory.—**R. Ruth Barton,** *Becoming Women of Purpose*

I see now that to live for God, whether one is allowed ability to be actively useful or not, is a great thing, and that it is a wonderful mercy to be allowed even to suffer, if thereby one can glorify him.—**Elizabeth P. Prentiss**

I wonder what becomes of lost opportunities. Perhaps our guardian angel gathers them up as we drop them, and will give them back to us in the beautiful sometime when we have grown wiser, and learned how to use them rightly. —**Helen Keller,** *The Story of My Life*

There has often been a tendency to think of service to God as necessarily entailing physical hardship and sacrifice. Although this is not really a Scriptural idea, it has gained wide acceptance. It is easy to recall the saints who climbed the steep ascent of heaven through peril, toil, and pain, but the Bible also makes mention of Dorcas whose service to God was the making of coats.—**Elisabeth Elliot,** *The Liberty of Obedience*

Our problem in evangelism is not that we don't have enough information—it is that we don't know how to be ourselves.—**Rebecca Manley Pippert,** *Out of the Salt Shaker and Into the World*

The world is full of lost people, motherless children and fragmented families who need our help. We can all participate in mothering, caring and nurturing. In such a way we fulfill our basic need to be needed, to reproduce ourselves in another by loving that person into the kingdom.—**Kari Torjesen Malcolm,** *Women at the Crossroads*

Christ came to give different gifts to different people. Some he made prophets; some he made preachers; some he made teachers. Since I have become a Christian I have thought he has given me the gift of being a sweeper. I want to sweep away some of the old difficulties that lie before the missionaries in their efforts to reach our Hindu widows.—**Pandita Ramabai**

If God has called you to China or any other place and you are sure in your own heart, let nothing deter you . . . remember it is God who has called you and it is the same as when he called Moses or Samuel.—**Gladys Aylward**

I am above eighty years old . . . I have been forty years a slave and forty years free, and would be here forty years more to have equal rights for all. I suppose I am kept here because something remains for me to do; I suppose I am yet to help to break the chain. I have done a great deal of work; as much as a man, but did not get so much pay. . . . I suppose I am about the only colored woman that goes about to speak for the rights of the colored women. I want to keep the thing stirring, now that the ice is cracked.—**Sojourner Truth**

I feel that God is calling me to do something for him I have not done in the past; that it is God laying upon me responsibilities I have not known hitherto; it is God pointing to higher heights than by his grace my poor feet have yet climbed; and it is God pointing to dark millions that before I had been only able to pray for, and not to help in so literal a sense as I hope to now.—**Emma Booth-Tucker**

For it makes but little difference after all where we spend these few fleeting years, if they are only spent for the glory of God. Be assured there is nothing else worth living for!—**Elizabeth Freeman**

It may be he has only sent me here as a stopgap. Part of a soldier's duty is to fill gaps, you know. One must as willingly be nothing, as something.—**Amy Carmichael**

Do not always look for gratitude, for, sometimes when you are most deserving, you will get the least.—**Ida Scudder,** address to medical school graduates

No, I will not retire, if by shedding my blood I can promote peace, why should I fly, now that the honour of Christ, and the peace of his spouse, are in peril?—**Catherine of Siena**

I felt a strong desire to obtain admission to the prisoners to read the Scriptures to them, for I thought much of their condition, and of their sin before God; how they were shut out from the society whose rights they had violated, and how destitute they were of the scriptural instruction which alone could meet their unhappy circumstances. . . . I did not make known my purpose of seeking admission to the jail, even to my beloved grandmother, until the object was attained, so sensitive was my fear lest any obstacle should thereby arise in my way, and the project seem a visionary one. God led me, and I consulted none but Him.—**Sarah Martin**

The power of organized womanhood is one of the most interesting studies of modern sociology. Formerly women knew so little of each other mentally, their common interests were so sentimental and gossipy, and their knowledge of all the larger affairs of human society was so meager that organization among them, in the modern sense, was impossible. Now their liberal intelligence, their contact in all the great interests of education, and their increasing influence for good in all the great reformatory movements of the age has created in them a greater respect for each other, and furnished the elements of organization for large and splendid purposes.—**Fannie Barrier Williams**

I wasn't God's first choice for what I've done for China. . . .
I don't know who it was. . . . It must have been a man . . .
a well-educated man. I don't know what happened. Perhaps he died. Perhaps he wasn't willing. . . . And God
looked down . . . and saw Gladys Aylward. . . . And God
said—"Well, she's willing!"—**Gladys Aylward**

Please give me those daily graces necessary to be fruitful
in virtue and good works.—**Marie of the Incarnation**

In the earnest path of duty,
With the high hopes and hearts sincere,
We, to useful lives aspiring,
Daily meet to labor here.

No vain dreams of earthly glory
Urge us onward to explore
Far-extending realms of knowledge,
With their rich and varied store;

But, with hope of aiding others,
Gladly we perform our part;
Nor forget, the mind, while storing,
We must educate the heart.
—**Charlotte Forten**

Universal and constant usefulness to all, is the important
lesson. And when we are fully and wholly given up to the
Lord, I am sure the heart can long for nothing so much as
that our time, talents, life, soul, and spirit, may become

upon earth a constant and living sacrifice. How I can be most so, that is the one object of my poor heart. Therefore, to have all the light that is possible, to see my way in this matter is my prayer day and night; for worthy is the Lamb to receive all honor and glory, and blessing.—**Lady Huntingdon,** in a letter to John Wesley

Social
Concerns

It will be a happy day for England when Christian ladies transfer their attention from poodles and terriers to destitute and starving children.—**Catherine Booth**

There are the "Robert Burns" and "Tom Moore" cigars. There was not a cigar in England when Burns or Tom Moore lived. . . . I never remember seeing the "Grant Cigar," by the way. His name is not used because he died with tobacco cancer.—**Carry Nation**

Patriotism in the female sex is the most disinterested of all virtues. Deprived of a voice in Legislation, obliged to submit to those Laws which are imposed upon us, is it not sufficient to make us indifferent to the publick Welfare? Yet all History and every age exhibit Instances of patriotic virtue in the female sex.—**Abigail Adams**

To make impossible the homeless conditions of incurable cancer patients; to make impossible their semi-neglect in homes that are unfit for them; to take the neediest class we know—both in poverty and suffering—and put them in such a condition that if our Lord knocked at the door I should not be ashamed to show what I have done. This is a great hope and may never be fulfilled by me.—**Rose Hawthorne Lathrop**

Epitaph on a child killed by procured abortion

O thou, whose eyes were closed in death's pale night,
Ere fate revealed thee to my aching sight;
Ambiguous something, by no standard fixed,
Fail span, of naught and of existence mixed;
Embryo, imperfect as my torturing thought,
Sad outcast of existence and of naught;
Thou, who to guilty love first ow'st thy frame,
Whom guilty honour kills to hide its shame;
Dire offspring! formed by love's too pleasing power!
Honour's dire victim in a luckless hour!
Soften the pangs that still revenge thy doom:
Nor, from the dark abyss of nature's womb,
Where back I cast thee, let revolving time
Call up past scenes to aggravate my crime.
Two adverse tyrants ruled thy wayward fate,
Thyself a helpless victim to their hate;
Love, spite of honour's dictates, gave thee breath;
Honour, in spite of love, pronounced thy death.
—**Anonymous,** 18th century

All of creation God gives to humankind to use. If this privilege is misused, God's justice permits creation to punish humanity.—**Hildegard of Bingen**

If we would build on a sure foundation in friendship, we must love our friends for their sake rather than for our own.—**Charlotte Brontë**

Give me your tired, your poor,
Your huddled masses yearning to breathe free,
The wretched refuse of your teeming shore.
Send these, the homeless, tempest-tossed to me,
I lift my lamp beside the golden door!
—**Emma Lazarus,** inscription on the Statue of Liberty

I leave you love. Injuries quickly forgotten quickly pass away. Personally and racially, our enemies must be forgiven. Our aim must be to create a world of fellowship and justice where no man's color or religion is held against him. "Love thy neighbor" is a precept which could transform the world if it were universally practiced.—**Mary McLeod Bethune,** *"My Last Will and Testament"*

The things which make men alike are finer and better than the things which keep them apart.—**Jane Addams,** *Twenty Years at Hull-House*

The greatest injustice done to our poor is that we fail to trust them, to respect them, to love them. How often we just push and pull.—**Mother Teresa,** *Total Surrender*

You have taken on yourself the wants, longings, desires of people, and you are bound not only to let them live, but to let them live happily; you must throw open to them stores of amusement, especially if they work hard, you must give them the power of learning; they must see friends, make presents, have holidays, and they will have the right to look to you for the power to do all these things; and if you do your duty, you will give it them, without their seeing it is any trouble.—**Octavia Hill,** to employers

When the national civil rulers enact more just laws, bearing equally upon all citizens, irrespective of sex or color, deepening and broadening the basic foundation of American government, which professes and should be non-partisan, and will give a strong guarantee that all its subjects shall be fully protected in civil and religious liberty, leaving each and all free (while law-abiding) to worship God in accordance with their own convictions of right and duty, irresponsible of any earthly tribunal, then the new earth will be formed, abounding in fruitful fields. Wars will cease, and fraternal relations between nations be established to the ends of the earth.—**Antoinette Doolittle**

We gave the invitation for all classes and conditions to come to the meeting. The invitation was accepted by the rich and poor, the white and the colored, church members and all kinds of sinners. . . . Some of the wealthy citizens said that they like the meetings, would help support them, but they would not do anything if we let the negroes come. Ministers and professing Christians said the same. They said all evangelists that had been in the city could do no good until they drove the negroes away. I told them God made the whole human family of one blood. Christ had

died for all. Christ said, "Go preach my gospel to all
nations, to every creature." Can we obey God and drive
the hungry souls away? . . . Thank God, amidst all this
trouble we shouted victory, knowing that God would
overrule all for his glory and do the greatest work ever
done in the State of Kentucky. I thank God we had no desire
to drive them away, but felt glad to have the privilege of
leading them to Christ. God came in such wonderful power
it was not long till they seemed to forget the color. The altar
was filled with seekers, white people on one side and colored
on the other.—**Maria Woodworth-Etter**

Thy gifts are, in respect to Thy goodness and free favor,
made common to all men, we through our haughtiness,
niggardships and distrust, do make them private and
peculiar. Correct Thou the thing which our iniquity hath
put out of order, and let Thy goodness supply that which our
niggardliness hath plucked away.—**Queen Elizabeth I**

Abolition! Prohibition! Suffrage! How we struggled for
these issues in Kansas. How simple and natural and right
these things seem now that the struggle is over. We did our
best with our problems. The result is the heritage we leave
our children.—**Fanny Holsinger**

Half the world is starving; the other half is on a diet. We are
not privileged because we deserve to be. Privilege accepted
should mean responsibility accepted.—**Madeleine L'Engle**,
The Rock That Is Higher

With what inward and outward respect must we not attend on those children when we consider the image of Jesus behind those disfigured faces and torn garments!
—**Jeanne Biscot**

Oh! slavery, with all its withering power,
Can never wholly quench the flame of love,
Nor dry the stream of tenderness that flows
In breasts maternal. A mother's love! deep grows
That plant of Heaven, fast by the well of life,
And nought can pluck it thence till woman cease
To be. Then, long as mothers' hearts are breaking
Beneath the hammer of the auctioneer,
And ruthless Avarice tears asunder bonds,
That the fiat of the Almighty joined,
So long should woman's melting voice be heard,
In intercession strong and deep, that this
Accused thing, this Achan in our camp,
May be removed.
—**Ada,** from *"Lines"*

That [man] says women can't have as much rights as men, because Christ wasn't a woman! Where did your Christ come from? . . . From God and a woman! Man had nothing to do with him. . . . If the first woman God ever made was strong enough to turn the world upside down all alone, these women together ought to be able to turn it back, and get it right side up again! And now they are asking to do it, the men better let them.—**Sojourner Truth**

Do you blame me that I loved him,
That my heart beat glad and free,
When he told me in the sweetest tones
He loved but only me?

Can you blame me that I did not see,
Beneath his burning kiss,
The serpent's wiles, nor even less hear
The deadly adder hiss?

Crime has no sex and yet today
I wear the brand of shame
Whilst he amid the gay and proud
Still bears an honored name.

Can you blame me if I've learned to think
Your hate of vice a sham,
When you so coldly crushed me down,
And then excused the man?

I'm glad God's ways are not your ways,
He does not see as man;
Within his love I know there's room
For those whom others ban.

No golden weights can turn the scale
Of justice in His sight;
And what is wrong in woman's life
In man's cannot be right.
—**Frances Ellen Watkins Harper,** "*A Double
Standard*"

I am afraid it is not human nature to be unselfish except in great crises. People look at things as individuals from an individual point of view, not from the point of view of history or the whole picture of the world.... Stop thinking for a little while. It is good for us all at times.—**Eleanor Roosevelt,** *My Day*

I would rather die of hunger myself than deny aid to the poor in this season, and thus become guilty of their death before God.—**Elizabeth of Portugal**

I can with more confidence ask of the Lord to grant me my necessities, when for love of him I have bestowed alms on the poor.—**Madame de Chantal**

I have received more from God than those people have received from me. He therefore gives me a great proof of his mercy, in affording me those opportunities of satisfying his justice.—**Madame de Miramion**

In refusing to do our best to improve and purify the social order, we are refusing the religious obligation to make it so far as we can a fit vehicle of the Spirit of God.—**Evelyn Underhill,** *Mixed Pasture*

It will be more agreeable to God if we nourish and preserve his living temples—human creatures—than if we spend to adorn this, his material temple.—**Jeanne Biscot**

I cannot know the real poor from the false; but God can, and he lets his sun shine alike on the wicked and on the just.—**Eleanor,** empress of Austria

My interest in the cause of prisons remains strong, and my zeal unabated; though it is curious to observe how much less is felt about it by the public generally. How little it would answer, in these important duties, to be too much affected by the good or bad opinion of man!—**Elizabeth Fry**

Souls are more or less securely fastened to bodies . . . and as you can't get the souls out and deal with them separately, you have to take them both together.—**Amy Carmichael**

No people ever rise higher, as a people, than the point to which they elevate their women.—**Isabella Thoburn**

While the spirit of neighborliness was important on the frontier because neighbors were so few, it is even more important now because our neighbors are so many. —**Claudia "Lady Bird" Johnson**

I discovered that it is not on our forgiveness any more than on our goodness that the world's healing hinges, but on His. When He tells us to love our enemies, He gives, along with the command, the love itself.—**Corrie ten Boom,** *The Hiding Place*

i think God does have wrath, but could it be kind of
   like justice?
i don't believe that weakens it.
justice stands
      immovable, for right,
and has no tolerance for wrong.
however long i live, i will believe
      though, that God, who is love, will always have mercy
   with His justice. He finds fault in us, but He does not
      tear down.
He seeks to bring love
         and to mend
         and to heal.
—**Ann Kiemel,** *I Love the Word Impossible*

We can help redefine the terms of family, love, and work. . . .
We must transform the nature of power and restructure
institutions for the sake of love of self . . . love of neighbor . . . love of God. . . . We can heal relationships and build
community. We can transform society by healing relationships of injustice and oppression.—**Elizabeth M. Scott,**
from *Women of Faith in Dialogue*

In the beauty of the lilies Christ was born across the sea,
With a glory in his bosom that transfigures you and me;
As he died to make men holy, let us die to make men free,
While God is marching on.
—**Julia Ward Howe,** *"Battle Hymn of the Republic"*

Sure the world is full of trouble, but as long as we have people undoing trouble we have a pretty good world.
—**Helen Keller**

When we ignore large segments of the body of Christ we are quenching the Holy Spirit.—**Kari Torjesen Malcolm,**
Women at the Crossroads

Biographical Index

Catherine of Genoa (1447–1510). Wealthy Italian mystic and author who served the sick and poor. *3, 24*

Catherine of Siena (1347–1380). Mystic and patron saint of Italy. *18, 19-20, 48, 53, 60, 125, 127, 135*

Cavendish, Margaret (1623–1673). Duchess of Newcastle. *33-34*

Chamberlain, Elsie (n.d.). *49*

Charles, Elizabeth R. (1828–1896). English author, translator, and hymn writer. *34*

Child, Lydia Maria (1802–1880). American abolitionist and author. *5, 95*

Christensen, Winnie (20th c.). American Bible teacher. *77-78*

Clare of Assisi (1192–1253). Italian coworker with Francis of Assisi and founder of the order of Poor Clares. *127, 129*

Clephane, Elizabeth C. (1830–1869). Scottish poet, famous for the poems set to hymns, "Beneath the Cross of Jesus" and "The Ninety and Nine." *59*

Colonna, Vittoria. (1490–1547). Roman noblewoman, poet, and intellectual companion of Michelangelo. *4, 114*

Crosby, Fanny J. (1820–1915). Blind American hymn writer of over 8,000 hymns and poems. *26, 34, 47*

Cruz, Sor Juana Ines de la (1648–1695). Spanish poet, writer, and nun. *67*

Cunningham, Sarah (20th c.). American religious editor and lecturer. *74*

Day, Dorothy (1897–1950). American journalist and reformer. *75*

De Chantal, Madame (1572–1641). French noblewoman and mystic who founded the Sisters of Visitation, and was canonized in 1751. *104, 148*

De Chardin, Marguerite Teilhard (d. 1936). French anthropologist and sister of Pierre Teilhard de Chardin. *51*

De Combe, Madame (1656–1692). Dutchwoman who opened a religious asylum for girls in France. *68*

Holt, Pat (20th c.). American school admimistrator and author. 87

Howe, Julia Ward (1819–1910). American writer and activist in the women's suffrage movement who wrote the "Battle Hymn of the Republic." 150

Hrostwitha (935–1002). Benedictine canoness and earliest known German poet. 74, 114-15

Huggett, Joyce (20th c.). English author. 102, 129-30

Hunt, Gladys (20th c.). American Bible teacher and author. 25, 65

Huntingdon, Lady (1707–1791). English Countess and patroness of revivalist George Whitfield and the Methodist movement. 39, 105, 136-37

Hutchinson, Anne (1591–1643). English-born New England preacher. 61

Isabella, Queen of Spain (1451–1504). Spanish queen who sponsored the voyages of Christopher Columbus. 61

Jackson, Mahalia (1911–1972). American gospel singer. 6

Joan of Arc (1412–1431). French saint and military heroine inspired by visions. 8, 77, 119

Johnson, Barbara (20th c.). American author and humorist. 19, 41

Johnson, Claudia "Lady Bird" (b. 1912). American First Lady (1963–1969) as the wife of President Lyndon Johnson. 149

Julian of Norwich (ca 1342–1413). Benedictine nun and mystic. 19, 37, 52-53, 62

Judson, Ann Hasseltine (1789–1826). First American woman missionary. 5, 90, 100

Keller, Helen (1880–1968). Blind and deaf American author and lecturer. 7, 13, 18, 132, 151

Ketterman, Grace (20th c.). American pediatrician and psychiatrist. 87

Kiemel, Ann (See Anderson, Ann Kiemel).

Kuhn, Isobel (1901–1957). American missionary to China. 11, 61

Lathrop, Rose Hawthorne (1851–1926). American founder of the Servants of Relief for Incurable Cancer. 141

Proba (4th c.). Roman aristocrat and poet. *115*

Quayle, Marilyn (20th c.). American lawyer and wife of former U.S. vice president (1989–1992) Dan Quayle. *9*

Queen Anne (1665–1714). Queen of Great Britain and Ireland. *65*

Queen Elizabeth I (1533–1603). Queen of England and Ireland. *51, 145*

Ramabai, Pandita (1858–1922). Educator and social reformer for women's rights in India. *40, 133*

Reapsome, Martha (20th c.). American Bible teacher and author. *36, 65*

Ridderhof, Joy (d. 1984). American missionary who founded Gospel Recordings. *54*

Rogers, Dale Evans (20th c.). American actress and author. *25, 64, 84, 91-92*

Rooney, Elizabeth (20th c.). American poet. *68-69, 106*

Roosevelt, Eleanor (1884–1962). American stateswoman, writer, and First Lady (1933–1945) as the wife of President Franklin D. Roosevelt. *77, 94, 148*

Roper, Gayle (20th c.). American author. *23, 79, 88, 96*

Rossetti, Christina G. (1830–1894). English poet. *32-33, 51, 53, 99*

Rowe, Elizabeth (1674–1737). British hymn writer, poet, and philanthropist. *56, 121*

Sayers, Dorothy L. (1893–1957). English author, playwright, and translator. *64, 66, 75, 80, 113*

Schaeffer, Edith (20th c.). American writer and speaker. *83, 92*

Schmidt, Ruth (20th c.). American educator and college president. *11*

Scott, Elizabeth M. (20th c.). American AME pastor. *150*

Scudder, Ida (1870–1960). American missionary doctor to India who established a major hospital and medical college. *134*

Seton, Elizabeth (1774–1821). American religious leader who founded the Sisters of Charity and was the first native-born American to be canonized. *6, 8, 18*

Shaw, Luci (20th c.). American poet. *66-67, 68, 76, 78, 92-93*

Shirreff, Emily L. (1814–1897). Hymn writer. *83*